FADING
PARTNERSHIP

Simon Serfaty

FADING PARTNERSHIP

*America
and Europe
after 30 Years*

PRAEGER

PRAEGER SPECIAL STUDIES • PRAEGER SCIENTIFIC

Library of Congress Cataloging in Publication Data

Serfaty, Simon.
    Fading partnership.

    Includes bibliographical references.
    1. Europe--Foreign relations--United States.
2. United States--Foreign relations--Europe.
3. Europe--Foreign relations--1945-   4. Parti
communiste français. 5. Partito communista Italiano.
I. Title.
D1065.U5S38   327.73'04   79-19755
ISBN 0-03-041816-X

Published in 1979 by Praeger Publishers
A Division of Holt, Rinehart and Winston/CBS, Inc.
383 Madison Avenue, New York, New York 10017 U.S.A.

© 1979 by Praeger Publishers

9 038 987654321

Printed in the United States of America

FOR GAIL

PREFACE

The history of the Atlantic Alliance is a history of discord and collaboration. It is a history that has been told many times: to review now the persistent sources of discord and to note the enduring commitment to collaboration may well challenge the reader's sense of *déjà lu* no less than the writer's fear of *déjà su*. Yet such "routinization" of discourse on the ups and downs of the alliance enhances rather than diminishes one's perception that substantial structural changes in the relationship between the two sides of the Atlantic are long overdue. After thirty years, the bonds between the Atlantic partners are fading.

For one, as shall be argued in the first chapter of this volume, the objectives, means, and purposes of the foreign policy of the United States have evolved significantly since the end of World War II. Initially faced with little international competition, the United States was easily able to equate the requirements of the West with its own: our own military and economic dominance made compromises superfluous. American aid, American protection, and American leadership came together, linked in a single package that had to be accepted as a whole or not at all. That aid and protection fulfilled their objectives—recovery and growth with security—most certainly shows that the leadership provided by Washington, whatever may be said and written of it now, worked well then. Indeed, the development and evolution of Atlantic relationships can and should be seen as one of the most impressive achievements of postwar U.S. foreign policy.

Such achievements, however, inevitably bred further discord and renewed competitiveness, for they permitted a new vigor in Western Europe, a vigor that, in the 1960s, stemmed from national wealth, political stability, and regional unity, if not from social justice and military strength. That the credibility of the U.S. dollar and nuclear deterrent should have begun to be questioned by the Europeans at essentially the same time is not surprising. What is surprising is that the ties between these two facets of European security—economic and military—should have been neglected for so long. What is even more surprising is that, 20 years after this first challenge in the late 1950s and early 1960s, the Atlantic system remains for all purposes unifocal as the European dependence on the American deterrent and the American dollar continues to be in full evidence, the French *force de frappe* and the German deutschmark notwithstanding.

Some, of course, find this state of affairs more than surprising. They find it deplorable. As the 1960s came to an end, perhaps too much was expected too soon from Western Europe. "In a wider sense, the European age has only begun," wrote Walter Laqueur in 1970.[1] Though about to pass away, the Gaullist torch had revealed a dynamism in Europe that, many thought, had not been seen since the pre-1914 days. But such announcements that Europe's agony had at long last ended proved to be premature. Every ten years, it appears (1949, 1959, 1969), the continent goes through a four-year high that a compelling necessity for unwanted choices—Atlantic or European?—soon ends: the demise of the European Defense Community in 1953-54; Nassau, Great Britain, and the Multilateral Force in 1963; the Year of Europe and the oil embargo in 1973.

The time now is 1979, a time for exuberance again—and why not? The prevailing gloom about the state of Europe that is sensed among most observers in the late 1970s poorly reflects, it seems, the various initiatives of European states in 1978-79. In the light of these attempts, a note of optimism may be in order—as will be seen in Chapter Five—even if written against a background of caution generated by the history of similar initiatives: for what external event might in 1982-83 dampen this timid and tentative resurgence of will in Europe?

While obstacles to such resurgence are numerous, it is to be hoped that not too many of them will prove to be raised by and from Washington again. As will be seen through the middle chapters of this book, the conflicts between Western Europe and the United States have progressively come to reflect genuine differences of interest. American military protection of Europe, once sought desperately, has descended to a level of secondary priority. European political emulation of America, once pursued feverishly, has come to face challenges from the left and from the right alike. Perhaps most of all, Atlantic economic relations, once consensual, have now become bitterly competitive.

History provides us with dangerous guidance. All too often, it may emerge as an insurmountable barrier to an adequate understanding of the present; all too often, it may blind us to the emergence of a new future. Looking at the alliance after fifteen years, Henry Kissinger warned, in *The Troubled Partnership*, against the possibility that a "nostalgia for the patterns of action that were appropriate when America was predominant and Europe impotent may become an obstacle to the creativity needed to deal with an entirely new situation."[2] In a way, he himself did not fully heed his own warning when he gained the opportunity to apply in practice what he had taught in theory. The warning, though, continues to be valid. Still in the making, this new situation need not harm American interests if we are willing to cooperate in defining with our allies what the permissible differences are, rather than attempt to impose on them what their legitimate behavior should remain, abroad and at home.[3]

NOTES

1. Walter Laquer, *Europe Since Hitler* (London: Weidenfeld and Nicolson, 1970), pp. 401-2.

2. Henry Kissinger, *The Troubled Partnership* (New York: McGraw Hill, 1965), p. 5.

3. Parts of this volume incorporate arguments presented by the author in various essays published over the past six years. These include: "The Kissinger Legacy: Old Obsessions and New Look," *World Today*, March 1977, and "Play it Again, Zbig," *Foreign*

Policy, Fall 1978, for Chapter 1; "America and Europe in the Seventies: Integration or Disintegration?" *Orbis*, Spring 1973, for Chapter 2; "Conciliation and Confrontation: A Strategy for North-South Negociations," *Orbis*, Spring 1978, for Chapter 3; "The United States and the Communist Parties in France and Italy, 1945–1947," *Studies in Comparative Communism*, Spring/Summer 1975, and "The Italian Communist Party and Europe: Historically Compromised?" *The Atlantic Community Quarterly*, Fall 1977, for Chapter 4.

CONTENTS

1

A NEW LOOK FOR
AN OLD WORLD?

THE KISSINGER LEGACY

The Nixon-Kissinger foreign policy administration viewed international relations as adversary relations. Whatever is thought of this approach, it permitted various policy adjustments that could still be regarded, by the end of the Kissinger era, as the first significant and sustained attempt to depart from post-war U.S. diplomacy.[1] To be sure, numerous New looks had been claimed or uncovered since April 1945. Yet, throughout that phase—the Cold War phase, as many have called it—there remained an impressive continuity of policies and concepts, a continuity that was nearly guaranteed by an overwhelming consensus that only the persistence of failure in Vietnam proved able to erode, however belatedly.

Such Cold War policies, and the support that they generated at home, had much to do with the image that the nation developed of itself in the course of its history. Repeatedly, the popular folklore that attributed to the republic global responsibilities rather than national interests was the focus of verbose great debates over what is, and what is not, realistic. In the 1960s, Vietnam, too, had been integrated into one of those debates. Thus, explaining it as more than a mere failure of policy, Henry Kissinger described the war more generally as a "very critical failure of the American philosophy of international relations." Kissinger was to recommend, shortly before he entered the White House, a reassessment of the "whole procedure and concepts that got us involved there . . . if we are not going to have another disaster that may have quite a different look but will have the same essential flaws."[2] There is no need to dwell once again on the intellectual mistakes of the former rhetoric. Suffice it to say that, devised to justify a given policy, such a rhetoric had ultimately emerged as policy within a framework that bore little resemblance to prior international and domestic

1

conditions. Earlier, entering the 1960s, President Kennedy, in his much cele-
brated inaugural address, had spoken of global objectives pursued through the
unlimited resources of a nation made even more determined by the perception
of crisis: "In [the] hour of maximum danger . . . [l] et every nation know . . .
that we shall pay any price, bear any burden, meet any hardship, support any
friend, oppose any foe to assure the survival and success of liberty." Kennedy's
pledge had been the logical completion of a process that had begun with Truman's Address to Congress in April 1947, when the new policies had been in a
sense formulated; the process had then continued with the outbreak of the
Korean War, when the application of the new policies had been tested; and it
had been accelerated during the Eisenhower administration, when the policies
had been extended through the signing of an entangling network of alliances.

Entering the 1970s, however, in the wake of a war that had emerged as the
dominant event of the previous decade, the very president who had done so
much to shape America's earlier policies was now recommending that the United
States turn away from old policies that failed. "The time has passed," Richard
Nixon pleaded in his second inaugural address, "when America will make every
other nation's conflict her own, or make every other nation's future our responsibility, or presume to tell the people of other nations how to manage their
own affairs." Each nation was said to have the responsibility of its own future
("We shall expect others to do their share"); and, while the United States remained willing to help ("We shall support vigorously the principle that no
country has the right to impose its will or its rule on another by force"), the
new structure of peace to which it aspired would be built on legitimate differences between systems of government. By so "europeanizing" the U.S. philosophy of international relations, the Nixon-Kissinger team assured, the United
States could balance means, objectives, and purposes in a way that would, they
hoped, satisfy the critics of the 1960s. In short, this new U.S. moderation would
signify the coming of a new look for a new world. "In an era of America's predominance," Secretary of State Kissinger reflected in April 1975, "America's
preferences held great sway. We could overwhelm our problems with our resources. We had little need to resort to the style of nations conducting foreign
policy with limited means—patience, subtlety, flexibility." But now, he continued, "we are one nation among many. . . . We must give up the illusion that
foreign policy can choose between morality and pragmatism. . . . No nation has
a monopoly of justice and virtue and none has the capacity to enforce its own
conceptions globally. In the nuclear age especially, diplomacy . . . often in-
volves the compromise of clashing principles."[3]

Subsequently reflective of these rhetorical adjustments was a reassessment of earlier, obsessive concerns with the ideological content of the cold war.
Not that in earlier years ideology had been made immediately an integral component of the nation's policies. Instead, up to 1950, with its foreign policy still
in a state of formation, the Truman administration hesitated in its appraisal of

Soviet objectives as well as in its assessment of the means that Moscow was prepared to use to fulfill such objectives—hence the occasional contradictions and apparent unpredictability of U.S. actions in those years: Czechoslovakia could go, but not Berlin; China, but not Korea. That Washington did not perceive initially the existence of one single Communist bloc was reflected, for example, in the support extended to Tito against Stalin, or in the reaction to Mao's victory in China, as the Truman administration continued to assume in early 1950 that national differences between two Communist states would soon outweigh their ideological affinities.

The Korean War, of course, changed all this. Intepreting both the North Korean effort to transform the existing status quo by force and the subsequent PRC entry into the war as proxy actions undertaken on behalf of the Soviet Union, the United States provided the elusive enemy with a coherence it could not have and ambitions that limited capabilities did not justify. Yet unrestrained and undifferentiated anticommunism was convenient given the mood of the nation at the time. It reconciled the country's genuine drive for harmony with its deep rooted instinct for violence. It provided the complex web of international relations that repelled most Americans with a much welcomed simplicity that appealed to most Americans. The enemy was everywhere, and its success anywhere was democracy's defeat regardless of the specifics of the situation. "International communism is a conspiracy composed of a certain number of people, all of whose names I do not know," warned John Foster Dulles in 1956. "International communism is still a group which is seeking to control the world."[4] What was wrong with this vision of the world was not so much that the Soviet Union should not be trusted, or that the Communists should not be acknowledged as legitimate partners in Western democratic governments. What was wrong was the global assumption that the only motivating force behind Moscow's foreign policy was its ideology; that the foreign policy of any and all Communist states was directed by and from Moscow; and that any force in favor of change was Communist, and, conversely, any force or group opposed to communism was, if not democratic, at least acceptable to other democracies. As empires crumbled, the United States failed to make the necessary distinction between communism and nationalism, and, unwittingly, led many to seek in Moscow what could not be obtained from Washington. As a new social consciousness emerged everywhere, the United States failed to make a distinction between revolution and evolution, and naturally emerged as the main pillar of a status quo that was being eroded by irreversible forces of change. Our own changes, whenever they did take place, came less out of wisdom than out of the evidence of failure.

Examples of such failures are many, and explanations even more numerous. This is not the place to list them. Yet, to repeat what became increasingly obvious, Vietnam was the outcome of a policy so defined. By the late 1960s, therefore, the time had come to draw the boundaries of our possible behavior—not only *what* we could do, but, even more importantly, for and against whom.

Thus, the Nixon-Kissinger New Look implied several adjustments in the U.S. response to Communist ideology. While, of course, communism remained abhorrent to the American way of life, it was progressively agreed that our relationship with such states was not to be denied on the basis of this ideological incompatibility alone; that Soviet influence over other Communist states varied widely from region to region, if not from country to country, thereby opening important opportunities that the United States could explore selectively and cautiously; and that any change anywhere was not always anti-U.S., nor was it always the successful result of a determined Soviet effort to expand its worldwide influence. "We must outgrow the notion," pleaded Kissinger in May 1975, "that every setback is a Soviet gain, or every problem is caused by Soviet actions."[5]

Although oversold at first by an administration anxious to gain public support for a shift that left many puzzled and concerned, the growing normalization of U.S. relations with both Moscow and Peking did not mean an instantaneous reconciliation of views among the national giants of the time. Instead, normalization followed a more hesitant path, still waging a Cold War, where and when needed, but without a Cold War rhetoric and while pursuing accommodation, where and when possible. Issues were linked, not always effectively, to form a chain reaction out of which an unbreakable net of new agreements might be woven between the United States and its adversaries.[6] In short, while adversary relationships no longer responded to ideological divergencies alone, they remained nonetheless relationships among adversaries. "We will react," said Kissinger on October 8, 1973, "if relaxation of tensions is used as a cover to exacerbate conflicts in international trouble spots. The Soviet Union cannot disregard these principles [of détente] in any area of the world without imperilling its entire relationship with the U.S. . . . Co-existence to us continues to have a very precise meaning: we will oppose the attempt of any country to achieve a position of predominance either globally or regionally." In other words, a relationship of détente with the Soviet Union in one area depended on Soviet restraint in other areas. Conversely, the absence of restraint would set in motion a process of action and reaction that would ultimately undermine the whole pattern of a U.S.-Soviet rapprochement.

It follows that in the early 1970s, the response of the United States to Communist ideology took one of three different forms, depending on Communist power and influence. Where a Communist government was firmly entrenched in power, as it was in the Soviet Union, Eastern Europe, and China (but admittedly not Cuba), the United States recognized it and dealt with it in spite of its campaign, privately pursued under the Kissinger-Ford administration, against the absence of human rights that continued to prevail in these regimes. Leftist governments that still faced substantial opposition from a disgruntled middle class, as in Chile for instance, were undermined by U.S. policies of "de-stabilization," which denied such governments the assistance they needed, even while Washington was extending to anti-Communist forces in such countries the assistance they sought. De-stabilization, however, was not based only on the fear that Soviet influence might grow out of the consolidation of a Communist regime in the area, as it had still been the case in the mid-1960s. More importantly, it was tied to the intrinsic appraisal of U.S. economic and strategic interests in the region, irrespective of Soviet gains. Finally, in those cases where Communist parties remained out of the government, the United States continued to state firmly its objections to change, as could be seen in Southern Europe, especially in Portugal and Italy.

On issues of physical security too, the Nixon-Kissinger new look tried to adjust to the changing military balance between the two major protagonists, a balance that had been evolving since the early 1960s. Throughout the Cold War years, the United States had attempted to maintain at first a nuclear hegemony that, on the basis of the most optimistic estimates, could not have lasted more than seven to ten years; and next, after such hegemony had ended, a nuclear superiority that would help fulfill James Forrestal's pledge that nothing short of 100 percent security for the American people was acceptable to the Truman administration or, as Forrestal foresaw it, any future administration. Given such an objective, the physical security of the United States could be assured only at the expense of Soviet insecurity, and the strength of one side dictated the terms of the other side's weakness. With negotiations legitimated only if undertaken on a position of superiority, the United States in effect demanded a recognition by the Soviet Union of its position of intrinsic military inferiority.

As such, then, Washington went through two phases of military exuberance, first, following the outbreak of the Korean War, when the initial atomic build-up took place between 1950 and 1955; and next, during the Kennedy administration when, on the basis of what may have been an excessive interpretation of Soviet capabilities and intentions, the United States accelerated the development and deployment of its own strategic forces. Former Secretary of Defense Robert McNamara has described well the rationale of such military obsession. "Security," he wrote in his *The Essence of Security*, "depends upon assuming a worst plausible case, and having the ability to cope with it. . . . Since we cannot be certain of Soviet intentions, we have to ensure against it . . . by undertaking . . . major build-up[s] of our own forces," whenever the possibility of a Soviet build-up is perceived at all.[7] Inherent in such reasoning was a self-fulfilling prophecy that had the Soviet Union actually do what it might not have otherwise done because of its own perception and understanding of the U.S. initiatives. Thus the Soviet build-up that Washington discovered in 1960 became a reality during the second half of the 1960s only, following the U.S. "response" of the Kennedy-Johnson years.

Ironically enough, it is, to a substantial extent, such an obsession with military superiority that helped keep the Cold War relatively free of direct military clashes between the two major protagonists. For, throughout the period 1945-60, both the United States and the Soviet Union carefully avoided overt military confrontation, in part, at least, because of the inflated fear each side had of the other side's capabilities. Thus there was at first a balance of illusions between the U.S. perception of Soviet conventional strength and the Soviet perception of U.S. strategic power. "What would it take for the Soviets to invade West Europe?" it was allegedly asked in the late 1940s. "Shoes," was the one-word answer: with Soviet land forces generously estimated at hundreds of divisions, the specter of such Russian hordes rushing through West Europe was a prospect that neither side of the Atlantic could easily contemplate. Yet it is now widely agreed that, in the aftermath of World War II, Stalin demobilized at a pace relatively impressive when one takes into account the particular security problems imposed upon the Soviet Union in light of its domestic and geopolitical position.[8] Similarly, the Soviet fear of U.S. strategic forces' preempting the Soviet Union is ironic when one considers that, by June of 1950, the United States was unlikely to have more than 100 atomic bombs with, by today's standards, uncertain means of delivery.[9]

It was only in the aftermath of the Korean War that the concept of a balance of terror slowly began to emerge. Such a balance, however, remained an illusion throughout the 1950s, as it was based upon a misconception on the part of each nation that the other could annihilate it, when in fact neither had adequate resources yet. For it is likely that by 1960 a U.S. preemptive strike upon the Soviet Union would not have had a reasonable certainty of inflicting upon the Soviets more damages than they had suffered from the Germans before Leningrad, that is to say, before they began to wage World War II "seriously."

Be that as it may, at his first press conference, on January 27, 1969, President Nixon clearly stated his preference for new criteria of "sufficiency", a term said to be more appropriate than either "superiority" or "parity". In a narrow military sense sufficiency meant the availability of force levels high enough, diversified enough, and reliable enough to inflict on any adversary an amount of damage that would deter it from attacking. In a broader political sense, sufficiency also meant to preserve for U.S. forces enough credibility and enough visibility to avoid any political intimidation by the Soviet Union (or China, or both) toward the United States and its allies. All in all, sufficiency downplayed the need to have more for the sake of sheer numbers, and even appeared to accept inferiority in certain areas as long as the resulting imbalances would be balanced. Central to this approach therefore was the assumption that there existed a point beyond which additional weapons lost either political or military significance as they permitted no further advantage for either side. The function of the SALT talks (initiated in November 1969) was to define and stabilize such "upper limits" of strategic weaponry.[10]

The earlier emphasis on "superior" military capabilities—"I mean first period," President Kennedy had once indicated, adding "I mean first in military power across the board"[11]—had come together with a rejection of diplomacy as an acceptable tool of conflict resolution. Now, it appeared, diplomacy was given a new legitimacy. In the past, as Adam Ulam has put it, "next to an all-out war, the prospect of negotiating with the Communists inspired the most fear in the bosoms of American diplomats."[12] This is not to say that negotiations were not held during the Cold War years. But the seeming objective of all sides engaged in those negotiations remained a maximization of satisfaction, which made an agreement, any agreement, unlikely. When taken at face value, such expressions and analogies as appeasement, Munich, credibility, or domino theory, basic to any analysis of Cold War policies, ended the search for a balancing of dissatisfaction even before the search could be initiated. If negotiations were to imply concessions, the Munich-minded policy makers thought, then negotiations would clearly also imply appeasement, thus reducing one's credibility and, in the process, opening the gate to either further concessions or war. Writing in the mid-1960s, Kissinger had sharply criticized such policy debates, which focused most passionately on whether to go to the conference room rather than on what to do once we went there.[13] In the 1970s, however, whether the United States should be in the conference room at all, and whether it should be there now, became less contentious: by the spring of 1975, 58 out of the 105 treaties and agreements that had been concluded between the United States and the Soviet Union since the former's diplomatic recognition of the latter had been signed under the Nixon-Kissinger-Ford foreign policy administration.[14]

Basically, détente meant neither the abrupt end nor the unhampered continuation of containment. If containment implied the nation's commitment to stopping Soviet expansionism, détente clearly added a strategy of inducement and absorption (primarily economic) to the former strategy of discouragement (primarily military). If it implied the nation's commitment to halting the spread of communism, détente certainly disavowed any pretense of rolling it back in Eastern Europe, probably reduced the national interest in the ideology of a given government outside the United States' areas of direct influence (in Asia and in Africa) and, as indicated above, confirmed the United States' unwillingness to tolerate ideologically hostile governments within areas of direct influence, namely, Latin America and Western Europe. Détente was meant to be containment without doctrine (that is, the Truman Doctrine) and at a deferred price. It was to entail the search for an ever-delicate balance between confrontation and conciliation with the Soviet Union—in admittedly unfavorable circumstances evolving from the perceived decline of U.S. leadership abroad (in the aftermath of Vietnam) and at home (in the midst and the aftermath of Watergate). "It makes a difference," Kissinger noted on December 12, 1975, "whether the Soviet Union is arming a country or whether it is arming a faction in a country. It makes a difference whether the Soviet Union is operating in an area of traditional relationships or whether it is attempting to establish a new pattern of dominance." These differences would be most vividly exposed during the post-Kissinger years.

Finally, a third aspect of the New Look related to the end of an obsession with an international system that, it had been believed somewhat too uncritically, would never end. Instead, in the early 1970s, bipolarity was at last said to be a thing of the past, forced into final retirement by the transformation of the Cold War system, as it had been known between 1945 and 1970. In Kissinger's words, "The post-war order of international relations ended with the last decade. . . . Gone was the rigid bipolar confrontation of the Cold War. In its place was a more fluid and complex world—with many centers of power, more subtle dangers, and new hopeful opportunities. Western Europe and Japan were stronger and more self-confident; our alliances needed to be adjusted towards a more equal partnership. The Communist world has fragmented over doctrine and national interest; there were promising prospects for more stable relations based on restraint and negotiation."[15] Not surprisingly, the emergence of a new world came together with a condemnation of the old one, now widely rejected as having been both an accident and an aberration. It had been an accident because it had implied the coincidental occurence at a given time in history of two events—on the one hand, the ascendancy of the United States and the USSR, two states whose rise had been foreseen since the early part of the nineteenth century, and, on the other hand, the collapse of the traditional European sources of power, whose decline had been watched for much time too. Furthermore, the old system was an aberration because of the very manner in which such an inevitable confrontation between the two remaining great powers took place. Seen in retrospect, and freed of the myths that the U.S. and the Soviet ideologies gave birth to, the Cold War was nothing more than a struggle for the hegemony of Europe, a struggle that had extended progressively to the rest of the world to an extent that was not always compatible with the best national interests of either side. Not unlike the preceding confrontations that had taken place in Europe for the control of Europe, this one too was bound to come to an end. As had been the case with similar conflicts, with the end of the Cold War came the need for a restructuring of the international system. Now, as then, the questions thus faced by the policymakers in building a new structure of peace were questions of membership, objectives, and procedures. If nothing else, the precedents of 1815, 1919 and 1945 showed that there is more stability in a system that aims at the balancing of dissatisfaction between allies and former enemies alike (as in Vienna in 1815) than in a system that aims at the maximization of satisfaction for the former allies (as in Versailles in 1919); hence, one would assume, the focus on adversary relationships.

But how effective was the new look in structuring a new system? For that matter, how new was the new world?

THE LIMITS OF THE NEW LOOK UNDER KISSINGER

Paramount among the problems that came to plague Kissinger's New Look were the uncertainities and ambiguities of détente. As a conceptualization, the triangle of détente was unquestionably compelling: similar in their mutual fear of each other, both Communist states were expected to turn to the United States and make the related measure of concessions required to secure some form of U.S. support against the other. Thus the holder of the balance, Washington could evenly distribute its amity to both sides in order to maximize its leverage.

Such a scheme, however, was easier to outline ideally than to apply practically. For one, both détentes were based on an initial and crucial misunderstanding. Peking responded to Washington's overtures in the hope of increasing tensions between the United States and the Soviet Union and gaining the assistance of the former against the latter. From a PRC viewpoint, Soviet suspicions of U.S. intentions in the Far East would generate additional conflicts between the United States and the Soviet Union, thereby raising more obstacles to an agreement between the two superpowers, an agreement that the PRC viewed as detrimental to its interests. Washington, too, wanted to use its nascent relationship with Peking to enhance its influence over Moscow. Such U.S. influence, it was hoped, would soften up the Soviet positions, and therefore facilitate the very entente which the PRC wanted to avoid. At the same time, it would reduce even further the possibility, already remote, of a renewed collusion between the two Communist capitals. In other words, while both the United States and the PRC saw détente between them as a means of influencing Soviet behavior, the former wanted this to result in a minimization of U.S.-Soviet enmity, while the latter wanted this to result in a maximization of that enmity.

With regard to détente between the Soviet Union and the United States, there was also an early and fundamental misunderstanding. The leadership in Moscow clearly understood détente as the recognition of the existing status quo in Europe, without, however, denying the permissibility of change elsewhere (especially in Africa, the Middle East, and even Latin America). Washington, however, wanted détente to permit a stabilization of the status quo in the various areas of superpower restraint that were periodically proposed, but without denying the permissibility of change in Eastern Europe (as the so-called basket three of the Helsinki agreement was expected to allow a progressive and graduated defiance of Soviet influence in Eastern Europe). To Washington, reliance on linkages and nets too easily confined détente to a choice between functional progression (peace by pieces) or global regression (peace in pieces); hence the gloom or exuberance that usually accompanied each setback or each accomplishment. Yet such a choice was to the advantage of the Soviets, who could use to their benefit concerns in Washington over the consequences of global regression in the light of the post-Vietnam mood of the nation. More often than not, the U.S. threat to link (that is, to join otherwise unrelated issues for bargaining purposes) could be dismissed by Moscow. To be effective, a linkage policy required the ability to sacrifice interests in one area to secure benefits in another. Such tradeoffs, however, became increasingly difficult because of the rising pressures exerted on the administration by the groups they affected most directly: the farmers and wheat deals, the manufacturers and trade talks, Africa and the congressional restraints, SALT and the liberal constituencies: who was linking what against whom?

Nor was the new rhetoric doing much to consolidate a domestic support for such a new look. With so many of its foreign policy illusions shattered in the course of a harsh and protracted debate over the Vietnam war, the U.S. public welcomed the opportunity provided by Kissinger's diplomatic method—his predilection for the personal and the acrobatic over the collective and the institutional—to slide into the more comfortable and more passive role of spectators. The peak of anti-Vietnam activism was reached in the spring of 1970; from then on, the distance between the war and the citizenry grew steadily. With this came a decline of interest in foreign affairs altogether, with a bottom reached by 1974, when the ten leading national priorities all had to do with domestic affairs.[16] Granted, then, that in the midst or the immediate aftermath of Vietnam it might have seemed incongruous for the United States to enter into a new crusade, still such prevailing sense of drift was not helped by the emerging subtleties (why shake Mr. Brezhnev's hand in Helsinki, and ignore Mr. Berlinguer's hand in Rome?), the emphasis on limits (one nation among many, to be sure, but one nation that had been born into the world to do mankind service), and the heretofore unknown pessimism (unbecoming to a nation that was still, by all measurable standards, the strongest, the wealthiest, and the most just).

In addition, the new rhetoric consecrated the breakdown of a domestic consensus that had grown out of a shared commitment to the world-wide containment of communism. References to the national interest opened the Pandora's box of vested and ethnic interests: against free trade that took jobs away; against an even-handed policy in the Middle East that betrayed the Israelis; against a strengthening of the Southern flank of NATO that sacrificed the Greeks; against an opening to Third World countries that did not secure the legitimate interests of the multinationals.

The U.S. public and the Congress could understand the meaning and implications of containment and superiority. They could not comprehend as easily the meaning and implications of détente and sufficiency. They deserted the very Kissingerian practices that they had applauded earlier: the secrecy that had framed the trip to Peking and the start of the negotiations with Hanoi was exposed as the source of covert actions in Cambodia, in Chile, and in Angola; the showmanship that had been so well received after the Rusk years was hurt by the sad spectacle of Watergate; the emphasis on the adversaries, which had resulted in the constructive initiatives of the late 1960s and early 1970s, was now seen as having damaged the more enduring relationships with the allies and caused the neglect of the Third World.

Abroad, the New Look found reluctant partners in détente. At home, it found a restive nation.[17] The very scope of Kissinger's ambitions in restructuring the United States' adversary relationships forced him to overlook the enduring influence of the past over the present. The magnitude of his achievements required a future to consolidate them, but denied him a present by exposing in the meanwhile the many flaws of such achievements. Foremost among these flaws was the place given to alliance relationships—especially the place of Europe, but also, of course, that of Japan and the other allies—in which case new policies proved to be singularly lacking.

Yet, early in the first Nixon administration, whatever there was of a European policy had seemed to reflect a new interest in Europe and even a new approach to the resolution of Atlantic differences. That the new U.S. team should have been initially well received, especially in Paris (then, as always, the most persistent adversary among the allies) was no coincidence. De Gaulle's leadership was effusively praised: "Of the leaders of Europe . . . he is the giant," Nixon reported, probably sincerely, following his European tour in early 1969.[18] The emergence of an independent European Europe was approvingly presented as a balance between the United States and the Soviet Union. The European commission and other community institutions were properly ignored, and the promise to avoid bilateral talks with Moscow was duly registered. In early 1969, de Gaulle could not have asked for more. But following such an auspicious start Europe was given little attention, and there could be found over the next few years no coherent pattern that might have defined the European policy of the new administration. Instead, a neglect of the Atlantic allies was appealing to the laissez fairists of the treasury (in 1969, the immediate monetary picture was momentarily reassuring and the year ended with a satisfying balance of payments surplus) as well as to the power realists of the State Department. All in all, it was reasoned, the many conflicts within the alliance did not lend themselves to any dramatic initiative. Placing them behind a rhetorical facade of Atlantic cohesion might therefore be sensible following years of public confrontation, especially at a time when, it was hoped, French nationalist obstinacy might be moderated following de Gaulle's resignation. Instead, however, such neglect facilitated a renewed European challenge to U.S. leadership. Charges and countercharges, freely exchanged by the likes of Connally (then secretary of the treasury) and Jobert (at the time the French foreign minister), took on increasingly bitter tones. These needed to be stopped: with the "acrobatics" on Vietnam, the Soviet Union, and the PRC well programmed, 1973 was therefore to be the Year of Europe, to face, as the administration saw it, the "new problems and new opportunities" inherent in such "changes in the international environment."[19]

Rather than the ultimatum that it was made out to be, the Kissinger proposal for an Atlantic Charter was a meager proposal. In a period of transition, Kissinger argued, the United States and Europe (as well as Canada and, "ultimately", Japan) needed a shared view of the emerging world. An Atlantic consensus on the prevailing "new realities" would then lead to the joint formulation of "new approaches" to Atlantic questions. It is such a consensus that the Secretary of State Kissinger asked the Europeans to help formulate.

That the proposal should have met with such acrimonious reaction in Europe reflected the gap that had grown, seemingly unbeknownst to the Nixon administration, during the previous four years. For one, Europeans had become increasingly anxious about the new intimacy between Washington and Moscow, especially following Nixon's state visit to the Soviet capital in 1972. To be sure, European statesmen could and did undertake such trips, as de Gaulle had done in 1967, and Willy Brandt in 1970. But this unprecedented visit by a U.S. president raised anew the charges of a nascent condominium between the two superpowers. "Europeans," Nixon had previously acknowledged, on March 4, 1969, while recounting his conversations overseas, "are highly sensitive about the United States and the Soviet Union making decisions that affect their future without their consultation." Europe's sensitivity over the consultative procedures of the alliance had been aroused many times before. In the first half of 1973 it was exacerbated further in areas of such vital importance as SALT I (Europe's general approval of the treaty notwithstanding) and the Soviet-U.S. pact on the avoidance of nuclear war in June of that year. Moreover, past dreams of European global influence had been revived in the 1960s, and in 1973 Europe was going through an ascending high that permitted little patience with Kissinger's condescending reference to Europe's "regional" interests, as compared to the United States' "global" responsibilities. For, prior to the crisis that would erupt later in the year, there was indeed nothing regional in the ambitions of a Europe that was growing both politically (from six to nine, with more to come) and economically (although strong inflationary pressures were already felt). Nor for that matter did Europe find the United States' fulfillment of its global responsibilities impressive: the Christmas bombing of Hanoi in 1972 was harshly criticized even by those in Europe who had previously displayed the most tenacious and consistent transatlantic faith.[20] Such renewed doubts about the hows of U.S. intervention—clearly distinct from earlier postwar concerns over the whethers of such interventions—encouraged further a bellicose mood of regional assertiveness. This mood was reflected, for example, in the pledge at the 1972 Paris summit to achieve union by 1980, by which time, some publicly foresaw, there might be a European government.[21] Looking at the future with such confidence, Europe found Kissinger's threats of linkages offensive, and rejected his argument that economic, military, and political issues were tied by reality. Instead, the Europeans wanted the Atlantic reality of security issues to be separated from the U.S.-EEC realities of economic and monetary relations, thereby leading ultimately to the elaboration of two statements of principles that, even if signed essentially simultaneously, nevertheless reduced effectively the consequences of linkage. "Partnership," said Chancellor Brandt in November 1973, "cannot mean subordination."[22]

The Year of Europe was expected to revitalize the Atlantic partnership in a changing world. Instead, its initial impact was to provide further momentum for European unity, a unity understood less as a component of a larger Atlantic partnership than as a rebellion against the U.S. hegemony in Atlantic policy. A specifically European view of world affairs did not facilitate the emergence—let alone the enforcement—of an Atlantic view. The Year of Europe therefore suffered an early and premature death as, with the end of the calendar year, Kissinger warned against a policy "to elevate refusal to consult into a principle defining European identity."[23] But by then the future evolution of the alliance during the Kissinger years was being shaped most significantly by events that were taking place outside the Atlantic area.

THE SEARCH FOR FOCUS: THE OLD AND THE NEW

Before examining the fate of the Kissinger New Look during the Carter administration, it is useful to address ourselves briefly to the question of a new world. That the two major architects of American foreign policy in the 1970s should have made of the global transformation of the international scene a major theme, both before and during their stay in power, is by itself significant. Such changes had been evident for many years, as successive waves of perceived or real détente (following Stalin's death in March 1953 and the Cuban missile crisis in November 1962) had combined with the economic recovery of the prewar centers of power (Japan and Western Europe) to legitimate a questioning of the postwar international structures.

Throughout the 1960s, Kissinger therefore spoke of the need to construct a new set of international relationships. This was said to be "the challenge of our time," not because the previous concepts had failed but because they had become largely irrelevant.[24] Thus he often returned to the warning that "the truths of one decade become the obstacle to the understanding of another."[25] Sharply critical of the rigidity of the 1950s, Kissinger advocated instead a tactical flexibility that he found to be especially lacking in the areas of U.S.-European and U.S.-Soviet relations.

In the 1970s, as a leading critic of the Kissinger policies, Zbigniew Brzezinski too had emphasized change. Thus, while drifting away from his earlier preoccupation with a Europe-centered system geared to the resolution of a basic

East-West conflict, Brzezinski had identified a North–South axis of conflict and cooperation around which a worldwide quest for equality was developing.[26] In such a world, Brzezinski argued, power realism was no longer a sufficient concept on which to base U.S. foreign policy. The new issues were different, born out of a technetronic age that demanded a concerted effort on the part of a trilateral alliance of the industrial states. Thus the Cold War could end with a claim of U.S. victory: with Brzezinski dismissing the Soviet Union as hardly even a rival of the United States, the United States was freed at last, freed, as President Carter put it at the very beginning of his term, "of [its] inordinate fear of communism."[27]

How new this new world was, of course, is open to question, not so much because there were doubts over the fact that shifts of historical magnitude had actually taken place, but because the long-term implications of these shifts remained difficult to measure.

Among the structural transformations most readily observed and tolerated was a redistribution of power and influence that, since the early 1960s, had been leading the world, however slowly, away from the bipolar configuration of the past, and toward a novel tri-multipolar constellation that Zbigniew Brzezinski once called a "2-1/2 + x + y Powers World."[28] The factors behind such a redistribution are well known: the still marginal but already meaningful relevance of PRC military power, which added an important constraint not only on the United States (in formulating its military strategy during the Vietnam war, for example) but even more on the Soviet Union (whose strategic posture was inevitably affected by its perception of PRC capabilities); the civilian recovery of Western Europe and Japan; the emergence of new poles of regional power with much influence among the less developed countries (Brazil, Iran, Nigeria, and Saudi Arabia); and the relocation of capital following the increases in oil prices in 1973–75, with the resulting reallocation of monetary leverage.

Everywhere in the world, but most notably in Africa, the competitive power of the "two and one-half" super states was overlapping with the renewed presence of former great powers, as well as with the self-assertive strength of the new influentials. Everywhere, too, new and implicit alliances of convenience were formed, often limited to the problem and objective of the moment. In the late 1970s, the ironies and the paradoxes that grew out of such diplomatic maneuvers—if not diplomatic chaos—were increasingly difficult to manage: in the Horn of Africa in 1977–78, when Cuban pilots were flying Soviet planes on missions against Marxist-dominated Eritrean guerillas (whose struggle was supported by conservative Saudi oil money) previously trained in Cuba and still using Soviet arms against an Ethiopian junta—once a recipient of American military assistance, now also engaged in a Soviet-supported war against Somalia, only the year before Moscow's best friend in the area;[29] in Indochina in 1978–79, when Vietnamese forces (equipped primarily with U.S. weapons) invaded Cambodia with the support of the Soviet Union but against the opposition of the PRC, their former ally, now aligned with the United States, the PRC's former enemy, in supporting a Cambodian regime reported by President Carter, only a few months earlier, to be a gross violator of human rights; and throughout Africa, where the most incongruous alignments could be found to contain and control what many saw as a potentially dangerous growth of Soviet-sponsored Cuban military presence and political influence in the area.

Such re-emergence of a multitude of independent actors inevitably caused a dispersion of enmity, reviving old, precolonial antagonisms and running the risk of causing new ones whenever and wherever this new power was co-existing with markedly weaker states. Where the former structures had been built around the U.S.-Soviet, East-West, conflict, first based in Europe, but, after Korea, enlarged to more global dimensions, the new structures appeared to be based on the intersection and interaction of a persistent East-West conflict with a more recent North-South confrontation, to which were added confused and confusing East-East, West-West, and South-South conflicts.

The rise of a so-called South, and its challenge to the industrial states of the North, was one of the most dramatic—and possibly least expected—features of the 1970s. Not only did it cause a historically unprecedented shift of resources in the direction of oil-exporting countries, it also emphasized the marked dependence of most industrial states on the raw materials of the less developed countries, a dependence that was measured not only in terms of prices but also in terms of security of supply. In earlier years, European countries had often argued with the United States over the need to preserve their empires in such a way as to prevent the emergence of such a situation. Now, however, although this dependence varied from Europe to the United States and Japan, and within Europe as well, every western country had become sensitive to a manipulation of economic and monetary resources by the countries of the South.

However, to focus only on the economic consequences of this dependence, or to reduce the demands put forward by the less developed countries to a search for additional resource transfers, mistakingly ignored the political dimension of the LDC strategy. The Third World now wanted more than economic aid and material well-being: it wanted a political autonomy and leverage that were to be gained by reducing the power and influence of the industrial states.[30] OPEC, of course, had been the catalyst for these aspirations. It had paved a way which other countries of the South might want to follow in accordance with their own capabilities. Yet, generalizing out of OPEC was made inappropriate by the many unique factors that had initially made the OPEC strategy so successful. Included among these were the political cohesion of the oil cartel, as most of its members were tied by religion and a common enemy (Israel); the indispensability of the commodity itself, oil, on which dependence was nearly total in a significant number of industrial countries, while stocks were very low and substitutes unavailable; the monetary reserves of several key members of the cartel (including Saudi Arabia and the Arab Emirates), which added to the credibility of a lasting embargo; the political disarray of the western states in 1973-74, as most of the governments then in power (those of Nixon in the United States, Tanaka in Japan, Brandt in West Germany, Pompidou in France, Heath in Great Britain) were weak and about to be replaced by new political teams whose stability and domestic legitimacy were, for a while at least, substantially improved (the governments of Ford, Mikki, Schmidt, Giscard d'Estaing, and Wilson, respectively). To speak of a North-South axis of conflict, therefore, exaggerated the cohesion and leverage of the South while it underestimated the ability of the North to exert pressures and create perturbations of its own. But such an axis also overlooked the significant relevance to these issues of an East-West axis of conflict, which no amount of détente could instantaneously eradicate.

As of 1977, the fluctuations of the Carter foreign policy reflected the dilemmas of an administration divided between its perception of a world that did not yet exist (assuming it ever would) and the realities of the world as it was still (some of these transformations notwithstanding). At Notre Dame on May 22, 1977, this was said by the president to be a new world ("In less than a generation we have seen the world change dramatically") that called for a new American foreign policy. Reflective of this need for a different approach was the Vietnam failure—"the best example of [the] intellectual and moral poverty" of the old policies. Symbolic of this change was the decline of the Soviet threat—"which once led us to embrace any dictator who joined us in that fear." Inspiring the new administration was the rejection of "the covert pessimism of some of our own leaders" who had not dared follow a policy "that the American people both support and, *for a change*, know and understand."

The new world was still present in Charleston, South Carolina on July 21, 1977—"a new world in which we cannot afford to be narrow in our vision, limited in our foresight, or selfish in our purpose," and in which the relationship with the Soviet Union, "however important . . . cannot be our sole preoccupation, to the exclusion of other world issues which also concern us both." Yet, by that time, the president was already being torn between the vision of a "gentler, freer more bountiful world" in which genuine accommodation could be achieved, and "the nature of the world as it really is," namely, one in which "the basis for complete mutual trust does not yet exist."

On March 17, 1978, at Wake Forest, the accent was placed on a different vision: even in a world that had "grown more complex and more interdependent," strength and resolve were required in the face of an "ominous inclination on the part of the Soviet Union to use its military power." By the beginning of June 1978 the change of focus was completed in Annapolis: the "world-wide political and military drama" called for "restraint in troubled areas and in turbulent times."[31] By finding in the absence of Soviet restraint the simplistic but convenient obstacle to the emergence of a system that was to be shaped by the various comprehensive plans of the previous year, the Carter administration returned to an analysis of the world based primarily on an East-West axis, the very axis, of course, that had been the basis of the Kissinger foreign policy. Condemning the attempts made by Soviet "marauders" to promote and exploit international difficulties, Brzezinski explained: "There are many different axes of conflict in the world. . . . They intersect, and the more they intersect, the more dangerous they become." References now proliferated about the Soviet use of so-called proxy forces, the need to keep the United States' number one position ("there's no way of knowing where you will stop once you start going downhill"), and the chaotic fragmentation that would result from an unwillingness on the part of the United States "to play an active role in the world."[32]

Where the new international system had further been seen as the product of a third phenomenon—namely, the devaluation of force—its evolution and stability were now made highly dependent on the extent to which the United States' will to use its power to balance that of other states would continue to decline further or would be revaluated with the consent of the American people. Over Angola, in 1975, Kissinger's plea had remained unheard in the name of this new world that was to be freed of coercion and inequality. "The phrase that the U.S. cannot be the world's policeman is one of those generalities that needs some refinement," Kissinger had argued on December 23, 1975. "Security in most parts of the world depend[s] on some American commitment." Without such commitment, he added in San Francisco on February 3, 1976, the perspectives of an international order that finds stability in balances and, ultimately, cooperation would be, to say the least, dim. Noting the coming of age of the Soviet Union as a superpower equal to the United States, Kissinger had also noted: "The emergence of ambitious new powers into an existing international structure is a recurrent phenomenon. Historically, the adjustment of an existing order to the arrival of one or more new actors almost invariably was accompanied by war—to impede the upstart, to remove or diminish some of the previously established actors, to test the balance of forces in a revised system." In short, the threat or use of U.S. force might still be required after all. In 1975-76, Kissinger's admonition had been met with a new round of congressional constraints that had limited U.S. freedom of military action to an extent hardly ever faced by a great power before. In 1977-78, over Zaire, a new administration, that included many who had applauded such constraints at the time, was ironically faced with the task of rejuvenating the credibility of U.S. power as a major ingredient of world order.

Most probably, then, such trends marked less the coming of a new age in international relations than the confirmation of the old one. While the United States was recouping from the Vietnam disaster and recovering its will to contain the expansionist challenge of the Soviet Union, other states were attempting to exploit existing opportunities at their periphery to improve their own status at the expense of others. Born out of the old, the new world was still ruled by the ancient imperatives of coercion and inequality: the United States and its allies would soon have to face the consequences of such realities or else suffer from the likely tragedies of their own delusions.

THE NEW LOOK AFTER KISSINGER

Hardly any postwar administration came into office as anxious as the Carter administration was to impress upon the public at large a sense of change in foreign policy. To be sure, in the midst of Korea and at the peak of McCarthyism, the Eisenhower administration too had wanted to present the image of new policies—rollback instead of containment, massive retaliation instead of limited wars, brinksmanship instead of alleged appeasement, to cite but a few. But such changes were meant primarily at the level of declaratory policies. At the level of action policies, changes were few and most of the Dulles initiatives of the 1950s were the natural continuation of the Truman-Acheson decisions that had followed the outbreak of the Korean War.

Policy makers, it is clear, inevitably inherit from their predecessors problems for which there is no immediate solution. To this extent, any one mistake is, as George Kennan once noted, "the product of all the mistakes that have gone before it, from which it derives a sort of cosmic forgiveness."[33] Yet, granted that the flaws and ambiguities of the policies pursued by the previous administration were numerous, the Kissinger legacy might nevertheless have been accepted in January 1977 as a relatively sound and stable one compared to the last three instances of orderly changes of administration (1953, 1961, and 1969). Indeed, with no war to be stopped, and for that matter no war to be waged, President Carter did not even inherit a public genuinely straddled with doubts over the role of the nation and anxious to reverse the perception of past failures through the elaboration of a strikingly new foreign policy. Instead, there appeared to be by the end of 1976 a renewed will in the United States to make its voice heard again, although with a measure of caution and without the excess of commitment that had characterized the Cold War years.[34]

Thus, if and when aroused, post-Vietnam but pre-Carter public interest reflected a keen preference for a tough, decisive, and, if needed, belligerent U.S. response to challenges abroad. Such an outlook might have been used by the Carter administration to promote the image of a self-assertive United States that had substantially outgrown the guilt and doubts engendered by the Vietnam War; that was again suspicious and fearful of the Soviet Union, its intentions, and its capabilities; and that therefore wanted to see a restoration of a U.S. power equaled by some but second to none. Instead, of course, the new administration proceeded under opposite assumptions that gave the Vietnam legacy more credit than it required. Or, to put it differently, the post-Vietnam era, which could have been terminated in 1977, was given a new lease of life by an administration that found in its numerous references to the lessons of the war facile explanations for various international setbacks.

It follows that the new administration proved to be unfortunately boxed in by its own previous words: the need to change was imposed less by the flow of international events than by the repeated pounding of the preceding years. Stimulated by the abstract rhetoric of the previous years (world order instead of balance of power, human rights as an essential part of the national interest, a comprehensive settlement in the Middle East instead of the step-by-step approach, the trilateral relationship as a substitute for the penchant for adversary relationships), the need for immediate change was aroused by personalities that enthusiastically sought fresh ideas with an inflated language that exaggerated the thought. Anxious to settle at once old and new conflicts alike, at home as well as abroad, the administration forced upon itself a comprehensive timetable with few priorities but numerous inconsistencies: a new arms control arrangement before October (and, later, added President Carter, "a final agreement eliminating nuclear weapons completely from our arsenal of death");[35] an accord between Israel and the Arabs before December (since this was seen as the most propitious time for a genuine settlement since the beginning of the Arab-Israeli conflict); accords in Southern Africa and Cyprus soon; normal diplomatic relations with such nations as Cuba, China, and Vietnam imminently; and, some day, human rights everywhere and arms sales nowhere.

In the midst of such early activism, much of the Kissinger legacy appeared at first to be rejected. This was especially visible in the evolution, from 1977 on, of the relationship between the United States and the Soviet Union. To be sure, a crisis between Washington and Moscow had been in the making before the arrival of the Carter administration. Excessive expectations about what détente meant and what it would deliver could not easily resist the tests of ever more visible Soviet activism in Africa, perceived communist gains in southern Europe, increased Soviet military expenditures, and much publicized domestic dissent in the Soviet Union. In addition to the substantive questions, raised by these factors (all in evidence during the latter years of the Kissinger era) the new administration was naturally seen by the Soviet leadership as less predictable and hence less reliable: the first few months of the Kennedy administration too had been characterized by a series of "tests" meant to measure the new president's will and domestic support—over Berlin and Laos, to cite but two of the more significant challenges that preceded the Cuban missile crisis of October 1962.

If, therefore, in 1977 the Carter administration could not actually be held responsible for the deterioration of the United States' relationship with the Soviet Union, it could nevertheless be declared liable for accelerating it markedly. For one, the public emphasis on human rights (which could have been expected by Moscow from the new administration) bewildered the Soviet authorities, who saw in it an orchestrated attack on their regime (as should have been expected by Moscow from the new administration. True, the Carter administration, while genuinely committed to the policy, nevertheless used it, probably unnecessarily, to rebuild for the time being at least a public interest the administration had thought to be lacking. This was the "creative vision" that Zbigniew Brzezinski had demanded a few years before, when it was indeed required, one that would be "capable of mobilizing the minds and spirits of peoples who sense drift but who are unable to define the needed response."[36] The United States during the 1960s had lost its sense of purpose, and what better purpose than the endorsement of a "historical birthright"—as President Carter called it—that made the United States indebted, in Madison's words, "to the world as well as to ourselves to let the example of one government at least protest against the corruption which prevails elsewhere?"[37] In so doing, the new administration wanted to rehabilitate at home a foreign policy that, it reasoned, Kissinger's eight-year seminar in power politics had much compromised. It undertook, in Anthony Lake's words, "an effort to harness a truly pragmatic approach to the service of traditional American principles," satisfied, in its own collective mind at least, that it would escape the self-defeating rigidity of the past, which had transformed principles into doctrine and had thus led to the tragedy of Vietnam.[38] Instead, it took the risk of forcing a new domestic rigidity over such questions of human rights, one that might prove to be equally self-defeating, as was shown in Iran in 1978–79.

There is no need to dwell at any length on the legitimacy of a human rights plank in the foreign policy platform of a great power. With the human rights campaign launched on the basis of items specifically related to the Soviet Union, it seemed illusory to assume that the Soviet authorities would take at face value the assertion that frank U.S. statements about injustice—made "from time to time" only, as Secretary Vance often emphasized—did not single out that country. Still, this marked departure from Kissinger's public practices might have been more tolerable from a Soviet viewpoint had it not come together with a hardening of Washington's position on SALT. Thus forced to be on the defensive morally, the Soviet Union was also being placed on the defensive strategically, as the early Carter proposals on SALT decidedly looked, and were, one-sided: an 18–25 percent reduction in the Vladivostok ceiling for total launcher numbers, with the sublimit on heavy Soviet missile deployment to be reduced by perhaps 50 percent. By setting as a ceiling on MIRVed ICBMs the very number of American Minuteman III, and by linking this with a low ceiling (six) on annual missile test launches (thereby reducing the potential for technical improvement), the United States was requiring the Soviet Union to make the sacrifices: Moscow already had over 1,300 MIRVed missiles and was lagging behind in accuracy.[39] As the Soviets felt so tested in substance and provoked in form, they inevitably asked themselves what stood behind the new administration's rhetoric. Was there truly a get-tough policy, or might the new U.S. president be a paper tiger who would backtrack from his foreign policy objectives as readily as he was already backtracking from his domestic objectives? Such questions—which had not been raised under the previous administration, whose "toughness" was more readily acknowledged by Moscow than it was in Washington—would ultimately lead the Soviet leaders to do some probing of their own to get answers that escaped them at the time. In this case, then, initial debates and disagreements carried with them the seeds of the more significant confrontations that unfolded subsequently.

On SALT and on other issues as well, most of Carter's initial objectives were, of course, commendable. They did reflect, however, a predilection for the desirable over the feasible that, as has been seen many times before, remains full of danger. A foreign policy of aroused expectations is a prelude to a foreign policy of crisis that results in a foreign policy of confrontation: the escalation is all but inescapable. Words develop a life of their own: used to explain or describe a policy, they soon become policy. So it was, not only with human rights but with other questions as well: on the Middle East and southern Africa, on arms sales and on China, the pronouncements remained far ahead of the achievements and the achievements therefore fell far behind the expectations generated by the very pronouncements of the administration.

Standing in Carter's way in 1977 there had been a fundamental misunderstanding over the status and role of the Soviet Union. To Kissinger, as we have seen, new approaches were necessitated by changing circumstances, both domestic and international. He, however, continued to acknowledge the Soviet Union as *the* major adversary of the United States, and, therefore, the East-West conflict as the basic conflict of the 1970s and of the 1980s. As the then secretary put it on December 23, 1975: "The basic problem in our relationship with the Soviet Union is the emergence of the Soviet Union into true superpower status . . . in the 70's and 80's. . . . In the past the emergence of a country into superpower status—such as, for example, imperial Germany vis-à-vis Great Britain—has generally led to war. Under the conditions of the nuclear age, it must not lead to war. . . . How to manage the emergence of Soviet power without sacrificing vital interest is the pre-eminent problem of our period. . . ."

This analysis had been initially shared by Brzezinski.[40] Thus, in the late 1960s, looking toward the 1970s, Brzezinski had perceived the future strictly in terms of the East-West conflict. While anxious to de-demonize (as he put it) the U.S.-Soviet relationship, he had warned that following the termination of the Vietnam War the competition between the two states might become more intense, less stable, and more global. "Power tempts policy," Brzezinski wrote then: even in the absence of a grand design, Soviet leaders could be expected to exploit quickly specific opportunities as they arose, especially in areas that were not covered by the same geopolitical imperatives as Latin America and Europe. "There is . . . no *a priori* reason," he pointed out, "to exclude the possibility that ten years from now Soviet marines could be landing in Nigeria or Ceylon."[41]

Thus taking for granted the continuance of Soviet international power, Brzezinski also took for granted the need for a continued commitment of U.S. power to the containment of the Soviet Union. "A panicky disengagement from world affairs because of frustrations spread by the Vietnam war," he argued, "would have a catastrophic effect on world stability," particularly in the less developed countries where, "at the minimum," one U.S.-Soviet confrontation could be expected.[42] Yet not only the very contradictions of the Soviet regime at home, but also the inevitable erosion of Moscow's dominance in Eastern Europe, would help meet the challenges of this "overlapping power." Such Soviet weaknesses had been discussed at length in previous works. In *Alternative to Partition*, for instance, they had led Brzezinski to the prediction that "placed high on the historical agenda [was] the likelihood that the Soviet bloc will soon share the fate of other imperial systems."[43] Consequently, policies had been identified throughout the 1960s to take advantage of such flaws in the Soviet military armor: a continued commitment to liberty as the best U.S. answer to Moscow's "increasing irrelevance . . . to the revolutionary processes of our age"; a differentiated policy toward Eastern European societies that would permit a selective internal liberalization of these societies, their gradual evolution into a greater Europe, and a pulling forward of the Soviet Union to the West; and finally, the effective use of Moscow's fear of some type of grand accommodation between the United States and the PRC. "A moderate China," Brzezinski had already suggested in 1968, "responding to cooperative overtures from Washington, could make the Soviet Union more aware of its stake in better East-West relations."[44] Accordingly, as would be more explicitly spelled out in mid-1973, Peking could make a significant contribution to the development of a more stable U.S.-Soviet relationship.[45] It would become—and why not?—the U.S. proxy against the Soviet Union.

In the 1970s, however, thinking Zbig had taken a different form, more opportunistic but far less prophetic. "How to deal with the Communist world," he wrote in *Foreign Affairs* in July 1973, "remains a key problem for U.S. foreign policy but it may no longer represent the central problem."[46] Imposed on both sides by opposite historical experiences and sharply different ideological perspectives, this competition between the United States and the Soviet Union was now, more than in the past, influenced by changes in the global context. The quest for equality on the part of the less developed nations—seen as the "underlying mood and the felt aspiration" of a growing majority of people around the globe—had become the moral problem of our time.[47] A foreign policy geared to the containment of Soviet power alone was therefore too narrow, and power realism was too delusive. However intelligently conceptualized and skillfully implemented, such a policy was historically irrelevant to the new

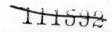

phase of the global political process.[48] Indeed, in shaping the new global relations, the Soviet Union, constrained by its own internal development, could
hardly rival the United States, whose role, conversely, was said to be "more
pivotal than it has been for over 20 years." Not to fulfill this role would result
in escalating chaos, as the task of key stabilizer could not be delegated to, or
seized by, any other state. "When America falters," Brzezinski concluded in the
summer of 1976, "the world economy and the political equilibrium become unstable. . . . The same happens to be true . . . strategically, especially in Europe,
the Middle East, and the Far East."[49] It is, of course, this latter analysis (that of
the 1970s as opposed to that of the 1960s) that proved to be the source of
Brzezinski's persistent calls for an architectural design for U.S. foreign policy
other than Kissinger's: "the need is not for acrobatics but for architecture"
(in early 1974); "what is needed today is a major architectural effort" (in early
1975); "it is only America that has the power to shape a hostile world for itself" (in mid-1976).[50]

There is little doubt that within the Carter administration such calls were
initially heard by the new president. Brzezinski himself was, after all, in his own
words, in charge of "influencing what is of central importance, namely the direction of things." For (still according to Brzezinski) the president wished his
national security assistant "to try to look beyond the problems of the immediate
and help him define a larger and more distant sense of direction."[51] Ironically
enough, it is precisely such a sense of direction that U.S. foreign policy proved
to be lacking most vividly by the end of the decade, as the Carter administration
now displayed an unsettling predilection for playing the juggler rather than the
architect. Much to its credit, the Kissinger New Look effectively checked the
post-Vietnam, post-Watergate decline of U.S. influence. Much to Kissinger's
regret, however, it failed to succeed in consolidating a domestic consensus that
would permit a renaissance of U.S. power vis-à-vis the Soviet Union. To Carter,
this was apparently not necessary: U.S. influence could be maintained without
tears by identifying those forces within the system, within each region, and
within the Soviet Union that constrained Soviet behavior.[52] Thus, the invisible
hand of such automatic containment picked out of Russian history the evidence
required to justify the defensive nature of the Soviet build-up; sought in the
underdevelopment of the Soviet economy and technology the comforting limits
that would necessarily impose themselves on further buildups in the future; and
found relief in the delegitimation of force in a world that applauded the U.S.
search for the equality of human rights.

Regrettably, assumptions of this sort belong to the realm of convictions
more than to the realm of realities. Granted that throughout the twentieth
century the history of Russia had been one of overall military unpreparedness
in the face of real threats—an unpreparedness that had resulted in the humilia-
tions of 1905 and 1962, as well as the slaughters of 1914 and 1941—still its
buildup, even if pursued at first for defensive purposes, came together with an

expansionist potential that U.S. history too had not escaped. The potential for Soviet expansion appeared in Moscow's accumulation of strategic and naval capabilities, which could hardly be seen as defensive in essence. Similarly, granted the relative backwardness of Soviet technology, there was nevertheless a sturdy, solid, reliable quality to its military achievements, achievements that were further enhanced by the operational diversity of Soviet forces. Nor could much be made out of the long-term inability of a totalitarian regime to keep up with this impressive pace of military expenditures at the expense of the welfare goals of the domestic economy. Still less was to be drawn out of the pervasive notion that, in the end, force was a thing of the past and human rights a reality of the present. For one, the relevance of military power was demonstrated not in its overt use but in its availability as a base upon which the desired political offensives could be launched. Without relying upon such a crude term as Finlandization, it remained true that the political shadow cast by military power could expand without drama, until the time came when it could no longer be rolled back without drama too.

In any case, the decline of force was a lesson drawn by the United States from its national experience in Vietnam. The Vietnamese themselves, soon embroiled in a new war with Cambodia, had apparently drawn different lessons from their confrontation with the United States. More to the point, a Soviet Union that had been forced to prudence by the U.S. superiority of the previous decades could now find it easier to release its energies more freely. Possibly, it might need a Vietnam of its own to test the effectiveness of its own military force. Where such a Vietnam would be was more difficult to predict than the likelihood of some form of U.S. involvement in it—unless of course, the United States was willing to opt for withdrawal altogether. But no one appeared to contemplate such an option seriously, as it remained neither feasible in the light of U.S. residual power, nor desirable given the United States' numerous and vital strategic and economic interests around the world.

Not surprisingly therefore, what had been initially most distinctive about the foreign policy of the Carter administration—the emphasis on human rights, the commitment to arms control, the tolerance of leftist nationalism, the acceptance of open debate within the administration—faded away as it came in contact with the realities of its environment, at home and abroad. The commitment to human rights thus became more selective, the search for arms control more prudent, the recognition of leftist legitimacy more hesitant, and internal debates more muted.[53] Now as before, and however reluctantly, the Carter administration, or its successor, would have to balance power with power, and, as predicted by Brzezinski in earlier years, new Fashodas would have to be fought. But balanced how, and fought among whom? While in the past the Soviet Union had acted effectively and ironically as a catalyst for Atlantic unity, the situation this time looked different. To some, while the Soviet threat was more real than ever, the U.S. protection was less credible than ever. The cancellation of the B-1 bomber, the Turkish arms embargo, the wavering and waffling over the neutron bomb, the handling of the SALT II negotiations, a noticeable willingness to pack up (Iran) and run (Taiwan): these and other, related issues raised questions about the quality and durability of U.S. leadership at a time when the costs of that leadership appeared to be increasing. As for others, whatever might be thought of Soviet intentions and U.S. protection, the real threat was elsewhere—in areas to which the actions of the United States had grown ineffective (access to raw materials at stable prices) or in areas where the United States itself was seen as the major culprit (money, inflation, trade). Rather then pointing to further Atlantic cohesion, therefore, the trend for the 1980s pointed toward a confirmation and exacerbation of past tensions; and even though the questions faced by the Atlantic Alliance all had a distinct air of *déjà vu* the answers that might be provided in the future could this time take a form of *jamais vu*.

NOTES

1. An earlier, and somewhat shorter version of this first section, titled "The Kissinger Legacy: Old Obsessions and New Looks," appeared in *The World Today*, March 1977, pp. 81–89.

2. Richard Pfeffer, ed., *No More Vietnams? The War and the Future of American Foreign Policy* (New York: Harper & Row, 1968), p. 13.

3. Henry Kissinger, Address to the American Society of Newspaper Editors in Washington, D.C., April 17, 1975.

4. U.S., Congress, Senate, Committee on Foreign Affairs, *Hearings*, 85th Cong., 1st sess., February 5 to February 11, 1957.

5. Henry Kissinger, Address to the St. Louis World Affairs Council, May 12, 1975.

6. Stanley Hoffmann, *Primacy or World Order: American Foreign Policy Since the Cold War* (New York: McGraw Hill, 1978), pp. 60–61.

7. Robert McNamara, *The Essence of Security, Reflections in Office* (New York: Harper & Row, 1968), pp. 53–58.

8. See Thomas W. Wolfe, *Soviet Power and Europe, 1945-1970* (Baltimore: Johns Hopkins Press, 1970).

9. See Simon Serfaty, *The Elusive Enemy: American Foreign Policy Since World War II* (Boston: Little Brown, 1972), p. 95.

10. See Kissinger's press conference of July 3, 1974.

11. Quoted in Henry Fairlie, *The Kennedy Promise* (New York: Dell, 1974), p. 64.

12. Quoted in Richard J. Barnet, *The Giants: Russia and America* (New York: Simon and Schuster, 1977), p. 17.

13. Henry Kissinger, *American Foreign Policy: Three Essays* (New York: W. W. Norton, 3rd edition, 1977), p. 87.

14. Alastair Buchan, "The United States and European Security," in *Western Europe: The Trials of Partnership* ed. David Landes (Lexington, Mass.: Lexington Books, 1976), p. 197.

15. Henry Kissinger, Address to newspaper editors, Washington, D.C., April 17, 1975.

16. William Watts and Lloyd Free, *America's Hopes and Fears—1976* (Potomac Associates, Policy Perspectives, January 1976) and Robert W. Tucker, William Watts, Lloyd

Free *The United States in the World . New Directions for the Post-Vietnam Era?* (Potomac Associates) Policy Perspectives, February 1976.

17. Hoffmann, *Primacy or World Order*, op. cit., p. 53.

18. Richard M. Nixon, News Conference of March 4, 1969.

19. Richard M. Nixon, *U.S. Foreign Policy for the 1970s: Shaping a Durable Peace*, A Report to the Congress, May 3, 1973.

20. Robert Schaetzel, *The Unhinged Alliance: America and the European Community* (New York: Harper & Row, 1975), p. 54.

21. Ibid., p. 2.

22. *New York Times*, November 14, 1973.

23. Henry Kissinger, Address to the Society of Pilgrims, London, December 12, 1973.

24. Henry Kissinger, "Domestic Structure and Foreign Policy," in *American Foreign Policy*, 3d ed., op. cit., p. 49.

25. Henry Kissinger, *The Necessity for Choice* (New York: Harper & Row, 1961), p. 65. Also, *Nuclear Weapons and Foreign Policy* (New York: Harper Brothers, 1959), p. xii; and *The Troubled Partnership* (New York: McGraw Hill, 1965), p. 5.

26. Zbigniew Brzezinski, "America in a Hostile World," *Foreign Policy*, Summer 1976, p. 95.

27. As stated by President Carter at Notre Dame on May 22, 1977.

28. Zbigniew Brzezinski, "The Balance of Power Delusion," *Foreign Policy*, Summer 1972, p. 54.

29. *Strategic Survey, 1977* (London: International Institute for Strategic Studies, 1978), p. 18.

30. Stephen D. Krasner, "North-South Economic Relations. The Quest for Economic Well-Being and Political Autonomy," in *Eagle Entangled*, eds. Kenneth Oye et al. (New York: Longman, 1979), p. 125.

31. President Carter's addresses at Wake Forest and Annapolis were delivered on March 17, and June 7, 1978, respectively.

32. See Elizabeth Drew, "Brzezinski," *The New Yorker*, May 1, 1978.

33. George Kennan, *American Diplomacy, 1900-1950* (Chicago: University of Chicago Press, 1951), p. 50 and 78.

34. William Watts and Lloyd Free, "Nationalism, Not Isolationism," *Foreign Policy*, Fall 1976, pp. 3-26.

35. As indicated in President Carter's speech at Notre Dame, May 22, 1977.

36. Zbigniew Brzezinski, "Peace and Power: Looking Toward the Seventies," *Encounter*, November 1968, p. 10.

37. Quoted in Paul A. Varg, *Foreign Policies of the Founding Fathers* (Baltimore, Md.: Penguin Books, 1970), p. 160.

38. Antohony Lake, Address before the World Affairs Council, Boston, Mass., June 13, 1977.

39. Richard Burt, "Reducing Strategic Arms at SALT: How Difficult, How Important?" in *The Future of Arms Control: Part I. Beyond SALT II*, ed. Christopher Bertram, Adelphi Paper no. 141 (London: International Institute for Strategic Studies, Spring 1978).

40. See my "Play it Again, Zbig," *Foreign Policy*, Fall 1978, pp. 3-21.

41. Brzezinski, "Peace and Power," op. cit., p. 9.

42. Ibid., pp. 9-10.

43. Brzezinski, *Alternative to Partition: For a Broader Conception of America's Role in Europe* (New York: McGraw Hill, 1965), p. 38 and passim.

44. Brzezinski, Peace and Power, op. cit., p. 9.

45. Brzezinski, "U.S. Foreign Policy: The Search for Focus," *Foreign Affairs*, July 1973, p. 721.

46. Ibid.

47. Brzezinski, "American in a Hostile World," op. cit., p. 67; Brzezinski, "The Search for Focus," op. cit., p. 717.

48. Zbigniew Brzezinski: "Half Past Nixon," *Foreign Policy*, Summer 1971, pp. 11 and 13; "The Deceptive Structure of Peace," *Foreign Policy*, Spring 1974, p. 53; "The Search for Focus," op. cit., p. 723.

49. Brzezinski, "America in a Hostile World," op. cit., pp. 93–94.

50. Brzezinski: "The Deceptive Structure of Peace," op. cit., p. 47; "Recognizing the Crisis," *Foreign Policy*, Winter 1974–75, p. 66; "America in a Hostile World," op. cit., p. 96.

51. Interview by Dom Bonafede, "White House Report," *National Journal*, October 15, 1977, p. 1596.

52. Robert W. Tucker, "Beyond Détente," *Commentary*, March 1977.

53. Kenneth A. Oye, "The Domain of Choice," in *Eagle Entangled*, op. cit., p. 26.

2

THE NUCLEAR FANTASIES

"The most desirable thing" that might ever happen to nuclear weapons, James Schlesinger once suggested, is that in the event of war, "they be destroyed before they inflict damage."[1] In the distorted world of nuclear fantasies, even Schlesinger's assertion—however reasonable it may be at a first glance—is questionable. In West Germany, for example, Bundeswehr analysts concluded in 1977 that a 20-day conventional war would be as costly as a 5-day war waged with tactical nuclear weapons.[2] At the most fundamental level, therefore, the difference for Germany between use and nonuse of such weapons is one of efficiency: everything else being equal, nonuse would not prevent, or even not reduce damage; it would merely delay it.

How to wage a war in Europe, at whose expense limitations can be achieved, and the impact of periodical changes in U.S. declaratory policies on such questions have been the object of innumerable discussions. In effect, the essence of the U.S. military contribution to the defense of Europe has never been merely the extension of economic or military assistance, the stationing of troops and related military hardware, or the convenient availability nearby of the Seventh Fleet. The essence of such contribution has been, as James E. King put it 20 years ago, "the extension . . . of the magic concession that an attack upon *his* territory is an attack upon *ours*, or at least that it will be regarded as endangering *our* peace and security."[3] Consequently, the essence of the strategic debate over the issue of physical security has referred to the credibility of such magic in the light of changing circumstances: if, when, where, and how U.S. nuclear weapons would be used to defend Europe, especially under conditions short of a direct and clear threat to the physical survival of the United States.

THE ATLANTIC SECURITY COMMUNITY

Alliances are what they become. Looking back to the original object of the Atlantic Alliance, as it was about to be formed, there was a common desire to structure a relationship sufficiently flexible to house the many security interests of the participating states. For France, for example, the entanglement of the United States into the affairs of Europe marked the successful conclusion of a diplomatic effort that had been initiated in the aftermath of World War I. "We have today obtained what we had hoped for in vain between the two wars," the French National Assembly was told during the parliamentary debate over the North Atlantic Treaty. "The United States recognizes there is neither peace nor security for America if Europe is in danger."[4] But danger from where? The French were concerned at least as much with the containment of a renewed threat from Germany, from where they had been invaded three times in four generations, as with the containment of Russia, whose expansionist instincts they had successfully managed historically. The alliance with the United States was seen and presented as the logical extension of the Franco-Russian alliance, which had been signed by de Gaulle in December 1944 ("two treaties with different guarantors," Foreign Minister Robert Schumann called them in April 1949),[5] as well as the natural expansion of the Franco-British alliance, signed in Dunkirk in early 1947. Both of these had an explicit German focus. For Italy, on the other hand, the alliance provided the anticommunist majority at home with the support (*punto d'appogio*) that was traditionally needed abroad. Thus, in his speech to the Italian Senate on March 27, 1949, Prime Minister De Gasperi dismissed the danger of an armed conflict with the East and argued instead that Italy's entry into the alliance would help "make the efforts of the international revolutionaries vain." It would also, of course, symbolize further the new legitimacy of the Italian state, whose re-entry into the concert of allegedly victorious European states sharply contrasted with the status of its former war allies. For Great Britain, the alliance was a way to combine her privileged relationship with Washington and her desire to remain associated with, if not a part of, Europe. The alliance would help control Russia ("We shan't reach any agreement but we shall live together," was Bevin's attitude),[6] and Great Britain would help control the United States. For all the neighbor states, alliance was a traditional guarantee pact, limited in terms of its specific area of application (neither the British nor the French were anxious to see U.S. interference in their colonial affairs) as well as in terms of its specific commitments: the automaticity that Paris sought was not granted by a treaty that preserved the usual escape clauses, while the dispatching of U.S. and British troops on the Continent (outside of the occupation zones) was not agreed upon until later. Neither side of the Atlantic acted as if it seriously anticipated an imminent Soviet attack. Indeed, at the hearings that preceded the overwhelming and bipartisan congressional endorsement of the first U.S. alliance outside the Western hemisphere in peacetime,

Secretary Acheson explicitly dismissed the possibility that substantial numbers of U.S. troops might be sent to Europe as a more or less permanent contribution to its defense.

The alliance resulted from a given situation at a given time. Reflective of this situation were the United States' strength and Europe's weakness. The latter, however, was not expected to last indefinitely, and the agreement was therefore reduced to a moment (25 years, although renewable), which Washington in fact would have liked to see shorter and Europe longer.

That the Europeans felt disconcerted over, and uncomfortable with, U.S. dominance is widely true, from country to country and across party lines. "Poor England," moaned Churchill while contemplating the leadership of the Americans. "They have become so big, and we are now so small."[7] Foreign Secretary Ernest Bevin speculated wistfully in October 1948, "If we only pushed on and developed Africa, we could have [the] U.S. dependent on us, and eating out of our hand, in four or five years."[8] The states of Europe in fact often appeared to be struggling among themselves for the control of U.S. foreign policy. The jealousy of the French over the closeness of London's association with Washington is a case in point: as early as July 1946, the then French Foreign Minister Georges Bidault was complaining that the United States was "incomparably more generous" to Great Britain than to France.[9] Even the Germans would soon boast of their ability to guide the behavior of a nation whose strength did not quite match, it was felt, its historical experience. "I firmly believe," wrote Foreign Minister Brentano to Chancellor Adenauer in March 1957, "that we largely have in our hands the capacity to determine American policy over the next years."[10] Also, woven into the early years of the alliance was, of course, the intellectual disdain that most Europeans displayed toward Americans. Norman Podhoretz captured the spirit of what it was like to be an American in Europe in the early days of the alliance when he reminisced over his first trip to the Continent in the early 1950s: "Being forced into a constant awareness of oneself as an American . . . , it was the American I stumbled upon while trying to discover Europe. For protest as we all might, the whole world insisted on regarding us quite simply and unarguably as Americans . . . in a million small details marked off in their eyes as an identifiable national type. . . . The sheer vulgarity of the anti-Americanism one came upon everywhere in Europe pushed many of us into the unaccustomed role of patriotic defenders."[11]

But the United States was not anxious either to see the dependence or the division of Europe go on indefinitely. With respect to Eastern Europe, it was hoped that the Atlantic structure would prove to be an irresistible pole of attraction to successive portions of the communist world, permitting, if not a direct absorption of communist states into the alliance (as it was considered in the case of Yugoslavia), at least a more or less explicit protection against Moscow's retaliation following disengagement from the Soviet orbit.[12] To this extent, rollback was indeed written into containment. With respect to Western

Europe, it was hoped that internal recovery (economically, thanks to Marshall aid, and politically, thanks to the ever larger anticommunist consensus that would result from economic growth) would combine with the unification of the Continent to permit the re-emergence of a force that no longer needed U.S. protection—an equal "partner" to the United States in its anti-Soviet ventures. An act of faith par excellence, the possibility that a strong and united Europe might be a competitor against the United States and that the time might come when the identity of Europe would be promoted all the more effectively as the influence of the United States was diminished was readily dismissed in favor of the logic of the Atlantic connection, a connection that would also control the potential for mischief that such a united Europe might gain.

As is well known, the Korean War transformed many of these assumptions. At once understood as a Soviet aggression by proxy, the North Korean action was said to set the stage for similar Communist aggressions elsewhere. Indeed, a Soviet invasion of western Europe was now expected by some as early as within two years. In the face of such pessimistic assessments of Soviet intentions, the fear of Germany was muted in an exceptionally short time: less than five years separate the announcement of the Pleven Plan, which was motivated by a deep mistrust of the German military, from the admission of Germany into NATO, following a bitter debate over the European Defense Community; and less than eight years separate Germany's entry into the western coalition from the Franco-German pact of January 1963. Thus, progressively relieved of the German threat, the alliance geared its efforts to the military containment of the Soviet Union. It became an integrated coalition army whose infrastructure concentrated specifically on deterring and defeating a Soviet thrust in Europe.

STRATEGIC CONTROVERSY IN THE ALLIANCE

It has been said that alliances are what they become; they are also what they do, or, in the meanwhile, what they might do. Now, throughout the 1950s, it remained relatively easy for western Europe to rely on the U.S. nuclear deterrent because of the clear superiority that the United States continued to enjoy over the Soviet Union, in terms of absolute numbers as well as in terms of technical developments. But by the end of the decade, as this advantage receded, and as the U.S. territory became increasingly exposed to the threat of a Soviet strike that might inflict a comparable level of damage, the United States found it properly necessary to adjust its policies in such a way as to insure adequate limitations should deterrence fail. Consequently, U.S. policy moved away from massive retaliation and toward controlled flexible response.

In 1961, the Joint Strategic Capabilities Plan (JSCP), which was inherited by President Kennedy from the previous administration, had contained only one option under which the initiation of war with the Soviet Union would be met

with an immediate and full launching of all U.S. strategic nuclear delivery ve-
hicles. In place of this single JSCP, various options and scenarios were devised,
to give a possible opponent, as McNamara put it at Ann Arbor in June 1962,
"the strongest imaginable incentive to refrain from striking our own cities."
Thus, for targeting purposes, the Soviet Union was separated from other communist countries (China and eastern European nations); distinctions were made
between strategic and civilian targets; reserves were preserved for intrawar deterrence; and special status was granted to U.S. and Soviet command and control
systems (to protect the former and to preserve the latter). The all-out "spasm"
option was kept last in a series of five options plus numerous suboptions.[13]

Western Europe's reaction to the new U.S. strategy was, to say the least,
skeptical. Articulated most consistently and critically in Paris (which saw in the
new strategy a U.S. attempt to deny the legitimacy of small independent nuclear
forces), such skepticism was generally shared throughout Europe. The McNamara doctrine, Europeans complained, was strategically dangerous (now told
that an attack launched below the atomic threshold could stay there, the Russians might find war more thinkable), politically self-defeating (by being so
obvious in its attempt to minimize the risk of using weapons to which the U.S.
mainland was truly vulnerable, the new strategy might revive the ever latent
mistrust of U.S. intentions), and economically wasteful (since it seemed to impose on the Europeans the burden of a further accumulation of conventional
arms that, it was argued, were unlikely to be of much relevance in a general conflict in Europe).

There is no need to dwell again on the further specifics of this debate; nor
to review once more the efforts made by the Kennedy and Johnson administrations to satisfy, insofar as feasible, European reservations. This has been done by
many others at great length elsewhere. Suffice it to ask briefly whether there
could ever be a U.S. (or European) strategy that might gain Europe's (or the
United States') favor. "I am prepared to conclude," a former high defense official wrote in the early 1970s, "that 20 years of efforts to find an acceptable
doctrine for the use of nuclear weapons in the defense of Europe have failed
because one does not exist."[14] Throughout those 20 years, and ever since as
well, the arguments entertained on both sides of the Atlantic, while exaggerating
greatly their own merits and the errors of the opposing arguments have nevertheless remain genuine; to this day, they remain unlikely to end in accord.[15]

Following the Korean War, the Europeans did not want to raise conventional armies, and they failed to take the necessary political and economic
measures to meet the goals agreed upon at the 1952 meetings of the NATO
Council (96 divisions, including a forward force of 35 to 40 divisions). Accordingly, they should have welcomed the handling of nuclear weapons as in the
category of "a bullet or anything else" (in President Eisenhower's phrase).[16]
Yet, when the 1954 meetings of the NATO Council scaled down the Lisbon
objectives and integrated nuclear weapons into NATO strategy as a compensa-

tory measure, the European governments now contended that given the inseparable location of civilian and military targets in western Europe, the use of nuclear weapons, tactical or otherwise, would prove to be so irreparable to European opinion as to invite abstention. Tactical nuclear weapons as Helmut Schmidt subsequently put it, "will not defend Europe but destroy it."[17] Throughout the 1950s, the Europeans wanted NATO nuclear pronouncements to intimidate the USSR through an emphasis on Western strength and resolve, and at the same time encourage European confidence by emphasizing Soviet weakness and prudence: consequently, they welcomed Dulles' rhetoric. Yet underestimating Soviet capabilities and intentions made European publics especially critical of the U.S. penchant in those years for superiority and brinksmanship: consequently, they also deplored Dulles' policies. Later, in the 1960s, with Soviet nuclear capabilities realistically estimated and the terrible contingency of nuclear war correspondingly taken into account, Europe criticized the consequences of the United States' justifiable attempts to limit damage: flexible response, it was said, would encourage Soviet aggression because of the decoupling of the U.S. deterrent that it might imply, in Soviet eyes, now or in the future. Europeans, who often appeared to uncover in both Washington and Moscow an irresistible urge of confining a war over Europe to Europe, often spoke as if they themselves would have preferred to limit such a war to U.S. and Soviet territories.

Underlying the Atlantic debate is a geographic asymmetry that cannot be overstated. Regardless of the strategy that is devised and ultimately implemented, geographic realities, one may conclude, render western Europe at its present level of military power more vulnerable than the United States by definition. Situated between both superpowers, Europe holds the same position as Poland held in the past, when a conflict between two of the great powers of the time, Prussia and Russia, was commonly resolved in, and at the expense of, Polish territories. The relevant realities of postwar Europe have included the proximity of the Soviet Union, thereby lessening significantly the time during which retaliation could be organized and launched; the distance of the United States, thereby complicating substantially the defensive cohesion of the Atlantic allies; and the physical compactness of Europe, thereby enhancing further its vulnerability to a Soviet strike. In practice, such realities could make it possible for both major protagonists to limit a military engagement between them to Europe (west and east) while keeping their own territories generally off-limits. "Who can say," asked de Gaulle at his apocalyptic best, "that if the occasion arises . . . [the Soviet Union and the United States] while each deciding not to launch its missiles at the main enemy so that it should itself be spared, will not crush the others? It is possible to imagine that in some awful day Western Europe [could] be wiped out from Moscow and Central Europe from Washington."[18] Then as now, no one could say, to be sure. Yet western Europe's reluctance to be wiped out from Moscow, possibly for the sake of Washington, can be matched only by Washington's reluctance to be wiped out from Moscow, possibly for the sake of western Europe.

There exists a security gap between the United States and Europe. However reluctantly, the search for security within the Atlantic Alliance has emerged as a zero-sum game wherein physical security for the United States could be sought, in part at least, at the expense of its western European allies. To strengthen the terms of deterrence, Washington must pledge its national body to the nuclear protection of western Europe. But to make defense possible, western Europe may have to relinquish its continental body so that the United States might survive a nonnuclear war. From the 1955 Carte Blanche exercise, which "defended" West Germany at an estimated cost of 5 million casualties in 48 hours (including 1.5 million Germans killed), to the reported "stalemate strategy" of a 1977 Policy Review Memorandum, which advocated a somewhat selective defense of western Europe at the cost of one-third of Germany's territory, the Atlantic dilemma has remained essentially unchanged.[19] What is rational on one side of the Atlantic may seem all the more irrational on the other, as either side might some day wish to lead the other into a war it did not want, for the sake of interests it did not share.

In 1957 Henry Kissinger had written: "The basic problem of strategy in the nuclear age is how to establish a relationship between a policy of deterrence and a strategy for fighting a war in case deterrence fails."[20] It is this problem, of course, that the Kennedy administration had addressed itself to, looking for a spectrum of *options* to meet, resist, and defeat Soviet challenges. Staffed or influenced by many of the academic and bureaucratic graduates of the early 1960s, the Nixon administration tried to deal with the same question, but from a follow-up perspective, namely, the need to develop a spectrum of *capabilities* that would permit the nation and its allies to respond to the previously acknowledged need for a range of options. "We must," said the president on February 25, 1971, "insure that we have the forces and procedures that provide us with alternatives appropriate to the nature and level of the provocation."

As an action policy there was little new in the subsequent Schlesinger doctrine that was publicly revealed in January 1974. When compared to McNamara's strategy, as it had been *stated* twelve years earlier, the main differences were in the renewed, public commitment to even more diversified clusters of options, as well as an official determination to integrate the navy into the new strategy.[21] More significantly, however, as a declaratory policy it served public notice on the Soviet Union that the United States was prepared to run the arms race along with Moscow, and thus sought from the Congress the additional funds required for that purpose.

Although tempered by the advances of technology, the contours of the Atlantic dilemma had therefore not changed much, in theory, since the early 1960s. Admittedly, because it would give the president additional flexibility in its range of retaliatory options, a counterforce damage-limiting strategy (one that would permit a response in kind to any sort of Soviet attack) increased the credibility of the U.S. deterrent before, during, and after the initiation of war.

But it required an overall U.S. superiority that might threaten to emerge, from a Soviet perspective, into a first strike capability which would invite Soviet reaction, as it had in the 1960s. Damage-limitation also increased the chances of war as both sides could now contemplate "victory" and "survival" following the initial exchange or exchanges. Conversely, damage-inflicting warfare reduced the likelihood of a nuclear engagement between the United States and the Soviet Union, as such an engagement might become irreversibly suicidal for both countries. But for that very reason, a countercity damage-inflicting strategy diminished the credibility of the U.S. deterrent should it be assumed, rightly or wrongly, by adversaries and allies alike, that the Soviet leadership was willing to take more chances than its counterpart in Washington. Thus, the question has remained unanswered: how to balance the requirements of deterrence with those of defense?

A U.S. strategy must altogether appear reliable to the Europeans, tolerable to the Soviets, and acceptable to the Americans. It must threaten the Russians without provoking them and without frightening the Europeans away. It must cater to the Europeans without compromising the security of the Americans. It must be plain enough to be understood by the American people, yet ambiguous enough to keep the Soviet Union off-balance. It must be sufficiently comprehensive to cover a series of contingencies that the most sophisticated and cautious analyst would not even have dreamt of a few years ago, yet it must remain cheap enough to remain economically acceptable to the U.S. Congress. It must strike a balance the terms of which defy one's imagination. In short, it is unlikely to exist: the physical asymmetry that prevails between the United States and its allies in Europe is not to be bridged through any formula, however vague, or doctrine, however imaginative. Herein lie the limits of Atlantic integration: the ever existing option to postpone retaliation for a moment of deliberation while the Soviet onslaught proceeds on the continent; the invaluable privilege to confine retaliation to the invaded territories of its allies; and the prospect to prepare their liberation from a home base, several thousand miles away, that is theoretically free of threat of occupation.

PROSPECTS FOR A EUROPEAN NUCLEAR DETERRENT

In Chicago, on March 15, 1974, President Nixon bluntly reminded the governments of Europe that "as far as security is concerned the United States is indispensable to the security of Europe, not only our presence in Europe but also the fact of our nuclear strength." But could such security never be achieved by the states of western Europe independently of the United States? Nearly 20 years earlier in Brussels, prior to the Suez debacle, Chancellor Adenauer had predicted that the extension of U.S. security for the peoples of Europe "cannot and must not become a permanent situation. . . . Vital necessities for European states are not always . . . vital necessities for the United States, and vice versa; there may result differences in political conceptions that may lead to independent political action."[22]

Behind Adenauer's remark (confirmed during the Suez crisis the following month, and repeated in various ways by so many others, government officials and observers alike) are the many quarrels that, even during its golden days, have characterized the Atlantic relationship: not only over Suez, but also Indochina, Berlin, and Algeria; over the NATO "directorate," the NATO "goals," and even the NATO "area"; about "shield," "sword," "tripwires," "triumvirates," and hostages"; about Finlandization (who is Finlandizing whom?) and adventurism (that of Stalin or Truman, Dulles or Khruschev?); about hegemony (whose?), special relationships (between whom?), and alleged condominiums (at whose expense?). Written into these and other quarrels is the question of a military autonomy for Europe that might permit the satisfaction of specifically European interests when these do not coincide with specifically U.S. interests.

Michel Tatu has called the devolution of power to Europe "a dream."[23] But is it a dream because of the insurmountable economic and technical obstacles that stand on the way of a credible, independent European nuclear deterrent? Or is it a dream because no such deterrent can exist until political integration has been achieved by the states of western Europe? Or, finally, is it a dream because even if such a deterrent might prove to be feasible, it would still fail to satisfy the security requirements of western Europe?

Surely, in terms of sheer economic capacity the Europeans countries have had a defense potential for many years now.[24] But with a GNP amounting to approximately four-fifths of the U.S. GNP, they have spent on defense substantially less than the United States. Accordingly, national efforts to develop nuclear forces have taken place thus far at the expense of conventional forces. Thus, Great Britain's 1957 White Paper placed a new emphasis upon the nuclear deterrent following what many regarded as the United States' treacherous abandonment of its allies over Suez the year before.[25] Given the prevailing pressures on reducing defense expenditures, this meant an alteration of the previous course toward multiple capability at the cost of conventional preparedness. Within a decade, however, as economic conditions made it impossible for Great Britain to maintain, let alone increase, its defense expenditures, the independent nuclear deterrent too had to be sacrificed, and Great Britain was left with military autonomy in neither the strategic nor the conventional realms. In France too, with the *force de frappe* responsible for nearly one-fifth (18.6 percent in 1971) of French defense spending, both de Gaulle and Pompidou had to penalize year after year other programs of re-equipment and force modernization. By 1976, the resulting imbalance in the defense posture of France was such as to have the French government introduce and implement a six-year plan that, the Gaullist objections notwithstanding, included a renewed emphasis on conventional weapons, while prior achievements in the strategic field were expected to be, at best, maintained.[26]

Yet, the cost of a medium-sized nuclear force is relatively modest, especially when compared to the cost of meeting high standards of conventional sufficiency. Even following the 1957 White Paper, Great Britain's expenditures on its strategic forces still represented less than one-tenth of its 1958 defense budget.[27] That same year, the amendment of the U.S. McMahon Act permitted some savings for Great Britain as significant data could now be exchanged between the two countries, and transfers of military hardware arranged. Developed without the benefits of U.S. assistance, the French force is therefore a more useful example of what an independent nuclear deterrent (weapons and delivery systems) might cost: between 1960 and 1971, $11.1 billion in capital costs (research, development, testing, production, and construction) and $1.7 billion in operating costs (personnel, training, maintenance, and operation).[28] If it is assumed that research and development expenditures occur primarily during the first decade of force development (in the French case, 1955-65), then it appears that from 1965 on, France incurred approximately $1 billion in average annual capital costs plus about $200 million a year in running and operating expenses—that is, 0.7 percent of France's GNP in 1971.

To assure an adequate protection of Europe through an independent nuclear deterrent would necessitate, of course, a force larger than the existing French force; it would not require, however, a force that would equal the size or the diversity of the Soviet or the U.S. forces. Instead, the distribution of Soviet population and industrial capacity is such as to make the requirements for a middle nuclear power rather small. Geoffrey Kemp, for instance, has tabulated that the assured destruction of the largest ten Soviet cities, including those (Moscow and Gorkiy) protected by the Moscow ABM system permitted under SALT I, can be accomplished with 11 sea-based delivery systems carrying 16 Polaris A-3 missiles each equipped with six MIRV warheads of 40 kilotons (with three more boats under conditions of "improved" Soviet antisubmarine warfare posture).[29]

The cost of such a seaborne force cannot be precisely evaluated. Surely more expensive than the French force (because substantially larger), it should not be underestimated, particularly during the first few years of its development and deployment. In other words, even if assumed by more than one state in Western Europe, expenditures would soar, especially if satisfactory levels of conventional preparedness were to be preserved as well. Likely to be under sharp domestic criticism, such expenditures could be justified only under circumstances of increasing international instability and, no less importantly, persistent uncertainties in Europe over U.S. reliability. Yet, current defense expenditures are not negligible either. Amounting to approximately $35 billion a year by the end of the 1970s, EEC defense spending is twice as much as the $17 billion that its NATO commitment reportedly costs the United States. What is negligible, however, is the amount of power (deterring or coercive) that is being purchased by the EEC countries for this price, as they remain subjected to the whims of their ally in the West, their main foe in the East, and their former colonies in the South. Seen in this light, there seems to be hardly any historical precedent of a state, or group of states, with both comparable defense expenditures combined with similar physical and human resources, and such total dependence on external support for security from physical aggression or economic strangulation.

Indeed, to question whether Western Europe has the economic means and the know-how required to build an autonomous nuclear deterrent appears somewhat ludicrous. However burdensome the financial costs might be, and however challenging the technological demands would be, the major obstacle to the feasibility of such a force is not the result of an absence of proper resources in Europe. What is missing more conclusively is the political will to do it. Undoubtedly, Europe's will, its absence of its rejuvenation, is a function of external circumstances. Predictably, as long as sufficient U.S. protection is extended by Washington, an activation of Europe's potential is unlikely to occur. Unquestioned U.S. guarantees tend to paralyze action, especially in a period of international détente that itself invites complacency. But, as seen in earlier years, much of the stimulus needed for a rejuvenation of Europe's will must also come from abroad. Thus, new military programs were legitimated in Great Britain after the outbreak of the Korean War, in France after the disaster in Dien Bien Phu, and in both countries after Suez. Similarly, the political re-launching of Europe has been in response to external events that spelled the impotence and isolation of the nation states of Europe—including the Schuman Plan, the Pleven Plan, and the Rome Treaty. Interestingly enough, while the European Defense Community (EDC) that was contemplated in the early 1950s as a response to U.S. pressures for a rearmament of Germany called for a European Political Community (EPC) as well, the EDC was to precede an EPC whose emergence was left for an ill-defined future. In the 1980s too, a European nuclear deterrent may not require prior political integration, and emerge instead around a loose intra-European defensive alliance, a bilateral (Anglo-French) agreement, or even one national force in the continent.

The French government has pointed to the existence of situations "in which France might feel threatened even before her own frontiers have been reached, in which case she would find it opportune to use her force of dissuasion."[30] What makes a regional extension of the French national sanctuary (*sanctuarisation élargie*) plausible, even if the transatlantic extension of the U.S. national sanctuary is doubted, is a geographic gap that makes damage limitation possible on one side of the Atlantic, while it remains impossible on the other. By European standards, war in Europe has become unthinkable. To be sure, this is not to be mentioned, let alone granted. Yet, the defense umbrella of NATO is accepted by Europe in bad faith as it is difficult to believe that in case of a major crisis between the United States and the Soviet Union, the European allies will unquestioningly and unanimously permit a situation to develop where they might literally be caught in the middle. In short, in Europe, there is no alternative to deterrence. Should deterrence fail, nevertheless, one doubts whether overt war, limited or not, nuclear or conventional, offers much of a choice to the Europeans themselves. "You probably would be liberating a corpse," the French already complained in early 1949, while seeking U.S. approval for a forward strategy for an alliance that had not been signed yet.[31] Whether regional or national, a nuclear force in western Europe would add to the credibility of deterrence because it increases the uncertainties faced by the Soviets in this new multipolar nuclear world—for no one would know for sure whether, in the last analysis, the Americans would not retaliate, or the Europeans, or even the French. In short, deterrence could be achieved for Europe by one or several European states together with the United States more credibly than it can be achieved for Europe by the United States alone. Whereas the political integration of Europe would be desirable, it is not indispensable.

Although free of a formal U.S. veto over its use, a European nuclear deterrent would not operate fully outside of the U.S. deterrent. Yet, such connection would surely be eroded if policy makers in Washington came to fear that the European deterrent might work as a strategic tripwire whereby a U.S. nuclear retaliation against a Soviet attack would be catalyzed by Europe's first use of its nuclear weapons. From the standpoint of the United States, this would invite Atlantic fragmentation as there would be serious concerns in Washington over the risks to wage a nuclear war for reasons deemed to be peripheral to the vital interests of the United States. From the standpoint of the Europeans, such fragmentation might cause a general *sauve qui peut*, that is, a frantic search for bilateral arrangements with the Soviet Union for some, neutrality for others.

Nuclear war, however, is no more indivisible than nonnuclear wars, and because the United States would still have the privilege of choosing isolation from a nuclear conflict involving the European deterrent, it would benefit from a collaboration that would help avoid such panic in Europe. With the balance of deterring power between the United States and the USSR at worst unaffected by the European deterrent, but at best possibly improved, the U.S. range of options would not be reduced, while Soviet policies might be inhibited by the multiplication of credible poles of retaliation. In any case, as seen in the 1960s with France, the emergence of an independent nuclear force in Europe in the face of U.S. hostility is harmful to all sides. To the French, U.S. opposition meant substantial additional costs (especially in the areas of research and development) and, at least for a time, political isolation. In turn, such isolation bred even more recalcitrance than de Gaulle wanted, culminating in his bitter departure from NATO, a departure that caused a further weakening of the Atlantic structures. Finally, the Franco-American confrontation led to considerable divisions and conflicts within the EEC, torn as it was between the French call for independence with questionable security, and the U.S. offering of security with questionable independence. Yet, U.S. obstruction and pressures did not prevent France from moving on with its program. Coming at a time when European countries see a reduced American will and diminished American capabilities to intervene on any one state's behalf, opposition from Washington to a European nuclear deterrent would be even less effective now than before. As perceived by the United States' allies, to oppose the proliferation of nuclear weapons *and* to preach the virtues of nonintervention is inconsistent, as the latter encourages the allies to seek among themselves, by themselves, or elsewhere whatever measure of security the United States no longer can or wants to provide.

Nor is the assumption that the dispersion of nuclear weapons to some states creates more instability for all states as self-evident as it is sometimes made out to be. Behind such an assumption lies the belief that the behavior of any new member of the nuclear club would be somehow less prudent than the club's charter members. This cannot be regarded as entirely persuasive in the light of current European aspirations. If and when used by the United States, an argument of this sort is an interesting reversal of prior concerns in Europe, whose "lecturing" of the United States on the seriousness of such matters has not been unfrequent—starting, for example, with the Anglo-French reaction to President Truman's warning, in late 1950, that atomic weapons might be used in the Korean War. To be sure, historical precedents show for Europe an imperial vocation that postwar U.S. foreign policy was anxious to control. Renewed military power might rekindle this European potential for mischiefs, were it not for the constraints that continued strategic inferiority vis à vis both superpowers will continue to impose on the Europeans for the indefinite future, that is as long as the European deterrent remains small.

West Germany, of course, is the state whose historical credentials are likely to be of special concern to all. Admittedly, there can be no adequate European deterrent without German economic support. Yet, the prospect of German participation in a European nuclear force would arouse the fears of the Soviet Union which continues to see the resurgence of West Germany's military power as the main threat to its security in Europe. This alone might provide Moscow with a sufficient justification for drastic action against the European deterrent, before it grows to any dangerous size, and regardless of the risks incurred. Yet, these risks are not insignificant. For one, there would be the ever present question of the U.S. response. Granted a reduced willingness in the United States to use its arsenal to protect states that would have sought their strategic independence, the possibility alone that there might nevertheless be retaliation from the United States would add significantly to the European assurances that there would be retaliation from western Europe. In other words, lingering uncertainties over U.S. policies would still encourage Soviet abstention, as may have happened, conceivably, every time the USSR has considered military action against the PRC over the last ten years. Indeed, since Moscow found that there was little it could do to prevent the PRC from acquiring and deploying a nuclear force of its own, why assume that it could and would do much more to prevent Europe-cum-Germany from doing so as well? There is no historical precedent of a Russian state seeking support in the East fo face a rearmed West (the Sino-Soviet pact of 1950 notwithstanding), but there are numerous examples showing the Russian willingness to tolerate a rearmed West when facing the threat of an arming East. Finally, large enough, as we have seen, to be used defensively as a force of dissuasion, but too small to be used offensively as a striking force, the European deterrent would be checked from within as well as the French would remain no less anxious that the Soviet Union (and, for that matter, the United States too) to control and contain whatever German aspirations may still exist.

The conclusion to be drawn from this overview is that in the coming years the question of nuclear forces in Europe not subject to U.S. control is going to arise again. How and when is, of course, not easy to predict. Accordingly, a U.S. policy that accepts to wait until the Europeans themselves find their way is all the more preferable as the strategic dilemmas within the Atlantic Alliance remain without any answer that would be equally satisfactory to all member states. When the time comes, however, it is to be hoped that a European nuclear force, if conceived in Europe neither against nor without the U.S. deterrent, will prove to be acceptable to the United States, if only since American opposition would probably be vain, and alternatives worse.

THE PERSISTENT THREAT

Beyond what the alliance is, becomes, does, or might do, stand the fluctuations of the threat itself. Not surprisingly, therefore, a main irritant of Atlantic relationships has been less the credibility of the U.S. protection than the questioning of the Soviet threat. The present shapes our re-reading of the past—who can say that Stalin ever intended to challenge the status quo in Europe?—and such rereading in turn erodes our vision of the future—shall we be condemned to repeating tomorrow yesterday's mistake? What is, then, the Soviet threat? Should it be defined in terms of stated Soviet intentions irrespective of Soviet power; or in terms of Soviet power irrespective of perceived Soviet intentions; or in terms of both, irrespective of the unreliable measurements that can be made of either?

The recent wave of literature on the early phase of postwar rivalry between the United States and the Soviet Union has helped shape a neotraditional interpretation that balances well the excesses of the earlier traditionalist school and the excesses of the latter revisionist school. Not surprisingly, such excesses parallel each other. Thus, the traditionalists exaggerated Stalin's military might and his leadership of a worldwide ideological conspiracy, as well as Truman's strategic weakness and altruistic intentions. The revisionists, on the other hand, made too much out of Truman's atomic power and commitment to the preservation and enhancement of an economic open door, while they failed to recognize sufficient relevance in the implications of Soviet military power and ideological influence. Yet, contemplating one another over the ruins of a devastated Europe, both the United States and the Soviet Union faced legitimate fears. For one, there was the awesome nature of the atom bomb as it had been demonstrated in early August 1945 and the overwhelming quantity of Soviet conventional resources as they had been released with the benefit of U.S. assistance during the war. To write now that U.S. atomic resources were essentially nil until the outbreak of the Korean War, or that the Soviet army was rapidly demobilized in the aftermath of World War II, is not to show that such situations were known then. Ironically enough, the U.S. illusion of Soviet power and the Soviet illusion of U.S. power neutralized each other and imposed on both sides constraints that helped avoid a military escalation of the political instability that prevailed at the time. Similarly, the communist ideology could easily take on a conspiratorial appearance following the re-emergence of the Cominform, the coup in Czechoslovakia, and the internal disorder in France—while at the same time the implications of such American initiatives as the Baruch Plan, the Marshall Plan, and NATO might have been seen from Moscow as a well-orchestrated attempt to keep Russia militarily weak, economically infiltrated, and politically threatened. In Europe, at least, containment and expansion described the same policy seen from two different perspectives. To point now to the many challenges faced by Stalin (from Togliatti, Tito, and Mao), whose ideological fervor was in any case much colored by his traditional perception of Russian interests (in Greece and China for instance), is not to show whether and how the disunity of the communist bloc could have been exploited at the time by the West more than it actually was.

There existed, in other words, an amount of military and ideological power in the Soviet Union the use of which was tempting to the Soviet leadership (be it for defensive or expansionist reasons) and containment of which was compelling to the U.S. leadership (for reasons that combined all at once the need for physical preservation, the imperatives of economic expansion, and the ideal commonalities of a shared faith in Western civilization). The fear of Stalin's power legitimated in western Europe the dependence on Truman's protection. What is paradoxical—with the benefit of hindsight—is that such fear and its resulting Atlantic solidarity should have been inspired by a Soviet Union whose relative weakness limited its objectives regionally, while, at a later time, a Soviet Union whose newly acquired strength enlarged its ambitions globally appeared to inspire relaxation and Atlantic disunity.

Already visible during the Korean War (but shattered somewhat in its immediate aftermath in Indochina), Atlantic solidarity was most impressive during the Cuban missile crisis in the fall of 1962. In many ways, such solidarity was surprising, coming as it did a few years after the Suez debacle and at a time when the Gaullist challenge to U.S. leadership was gaining a momentum that would soon lead to France's departure from NATO. Yet the relocation of what was then a significant portion of Soviet strategic power into the U.S. security area was understood to be an unquestionable attempt on the part of the Soviet leadership to modify the existing balance of power between the two super-powers. This had ominous implications for the security of western Europe, especially at a time when Moscow was aggressively engaged in a power play over Berlin. The Cuban missile crisis was therefore an effort by the West—surely the most dramatic, if not the last—to preserve its strategic superiority over the Soviet Union, by force if necessary. Its success, needless to say, was of short duration: exactly seven years later the opening of the SALT negotiations signified acknowl-edgement by the United States that its commitment to strategic superiority had come to an end, and that the parameters of parity now needed to be better de-fined if the resulting balance was to be stabilized at all.

In obvious opposition to the solidarity shown over Cuba in 1962 stands the disunity shown during the war in the Middle East in late 1973:[32] the state-ments of neutrality by several NATO members; Turkey's acquiescence in the overflight of its territory by the Soviet arms airlift to the Arabs; the public pro-hibition by Turkey, but also by Greece and Italy (as well as Spain), of landing in or overflying these territories for a similar arms lift to Israel; a parallel, although less demonstrative, prohibition by Great Britain and West Germany. Europe's skepticism toward the United States' policy during the crisis culminated, of course, with the widely and openly displayed doubts over the measures taken by Washington on October 25 to counter any unilateral Soviet move in the area: where Europe had found it unnecessary to consider the evidence in 1962, it now dismissed as irrelevant the presentation of any such evidence of possible Soviet military intervention in the area—an area of obvious strategic and eco-nomic importance to Europe, one, indeed, over which Great Britain and France had last been willing to go to war 17 years earlier.

While the solidarity of NATO in areas going beyond the geographic scope of the treaty has been diminishing, Soviet power in all areas has been growing considerably. As we have seen, in the 1950s and during much of the 1960s the relative absence of actual Soviet power caused a concern with Soviet intentions all the more acute as the Soviet leadership often dramatized its own rhetoric: witness, for example, Khrushchev's frequent reliance on nuclear blackmail in 1956-62, at the very time U.S. strategic superiority was increasing. Such threats were in fact often addressed to the United States. Thus, on September 7, 1958, at the height of a crisis over the islands of Quemoy and Matsu, Khrushchev pointedly observed in a letter to Eisenhower that the ships of the Seventh Fleet in the Formosa Straits "can serve as targets for the right kinds of rockets."[33]

There is little doubt that from the mid-1960s on the real concern moved away from perceived intentions toward actual capabilities, as the strategic balance between the United States and the Soviet Union began to shift to a situation said to be of rough equivalency, with, however, a threatening potential for future Soviet superiority. That such potential seemed to be hardly hampered by the SALT negotiations made such concern all the more real. All in all, by early 1978, the United States appeared to enjoy continued, though diminishing, advantages in numbers of deliverable warheads (nearly three to one), equivalent megatonnage (about three to two), missile accuracies, bomber payloads (approximately five to one), and electronic countermeasures for bombers. The Soviets, on the other hand, enjoyed substantial quantitative superiority in areas of high political visibility (especially intercontinental ballistic missles) as well as a significant missile throw-weight advantage (nearly three to one) due to their predilection for heavy missiles and larger silos.

Similarly, direct comparisons of the NATO/U.S. combat capabilities in Europe with the Warsaw Pact/USSR totals provided the image of a militarily dynamic East slowly overtaking an often reluctant and occasionally divided West. Where in 1962 the U.S. land, sea, and air forces in Europe totaled 434,000, the figure in 1977 was about 300,000. Meanwhile, the 26 Soviet divisions found in Eastern Europe in 1967 had been increased, by 1977, to 31 divisions, of greater size. In the area of confrontation in central Europe, NATO had 734,000 troops, 6,430 tanks, 1,700 tactical aircrafts, and 7,000 tactical nuclear warheads; the Warsaw Pact forces included approximately 900,000 troops, 15,700 tanks, 3,000 tactical aircrafts, and 3,500 tactical nuclear warheads.[34] Such theater-wide accounts, however, helped dissimulate harsher truths: even if the southwest of Germany could be held by NATO forces in the area, it remained "beyond the skill of any scenario designer" to show how the north of Germany could be held as well.[35]

Finally, to make matters more difficult, the Warsaw Pact has remained a centralized and Soviet-controlled system, equipped nearly entirely with Soviet or Soviet-designed materials, and has enjoyed the flexibility, simplicity of training, and economy that such standardization permits. NATO, by contrast, continues to be subject to the conflicting pressures of different national governments, suffers from an inflexible logistic system, based almost entirely on national supply lines with little central coordination, and relies, in spite of the many genuine efforts and real improvements of the 1970s, on a wide variety of weapons systems with consequent duplication and problems of interoperability.[36]

In sum, numbers, organization, and geography increasingly favor the East at a time when the former advantages of the West (technology and motivation) have consistently diminished. With respect to a larger and increasing number of military items, the expansion of Soviet forces has enabled Moscow to move ahead of the United States, achieve rough equality, or render the gap insignificant. At the same time, however, the earlier expectation that Soviet numerical advantages would be balanced by continued U.S. technical superiority has been denied either by steady Soviet improvements (in missile accuracy, for example) or by a persisting U.S. reluctance to deploy those systems that might have helped preserve such advantage: the Bl, for instance, was admittedly a more impressive penetrating bomber than Moscow's Backfire—but where the latter is being made operational, the former has been held back by the Carter adminis-tration.

This is not to say that, by the late 1970s, U.S. and NATO forces were no longer sufficient to impose upon the Soviet Union strict limitations on their actions in and against Europe. It is to say, however, that, regardless of the index of strategic capabilities used, the direction and pace of change during the pre-vious years, if projected into the 1980s, pointed to an impressive shift in the military balance in favor of the Soviet Union. If pursued, such a trend might make it possible for the Soviet Union and its allies to neutralize U.S. strategic forces while preserving, if not enhancing, their conventional supremacy. In the past, it was U.S. superiority in the nuclear arena that had effectively balanced such Soviet conventional advantages. It gave NATO a so-called escalation domi-nance, whereby the threat to escalate a conventional conflict into a nuclear war was a threat directed by the United States to the Soviet Union even if U.S. cities were vulnerable to Soviet retaliation.[37] The alliance's shield was linked to the U.S. sword, thanks to a nuclear component the size of which, by the early 1960s, reflected the awesome production capacity of the U.S. economy. Now, however, the Soviets could theoretically contemplate a longer conventional en-gagement in a military offensive in Europe: given the emerging military balance, the relative weight of U.S. nuclear forces had diminished. All too dramatically, the deterrent could be said to be itself on the verge of being deterred, as a funda-mental leg of the U.S. triad—the land-based ballistic missiles—might soon be ex-posed to pre-emption by the Soviet Union with a reasonable measure of cer-tainty and at a small cost of the Soviet missile forces.[38]

Without reviewing again the details of these doomsday scenarios, nor arguing once more over the specifics of the SALT II negotiations, it is im-portant to note that throughout the latter part of the 1970s Europe grew in-creasingly sensitive to the U.S. acquiescence of, if not indifference to, Soviet strategic advances. Year by year, improvements in the Soviet posture had come slowly, as defense planners in Moscow continued to emphasize what they did best, even while they were learning to do more and more better. This absence of drama, many in Europe feared, had helped lure the U.S. citizenry into a false sense of complacency over issues of physical security. But this public com-placency (although disrupted by such events as the unpredicted upheaval in Iran) had itself been promoted by two successive administrations in Washington that found it repeatedly necessary to soft pedal whatever reservations they had about Soviet intentions while they praised effusively whatever concessions the Soviets made to secure an elusive congressional approval for the SALT II treaty and future SALT III negotiations. Seen from Europe, therefore, the support re-ported among the general American public for SALT II was especially surprising in view of the many genuine questions raised about the accord by congressional critics in Washington.

The Soviet ability to impress upon the major allies of the United States, that the once dominant power of their protector might no longer be credible (and, some day, might no longer be sufficient) was enhanced not only by the tangibles of the Soviet military buildup but also by the intangibles of the United States' own uncertainties and, hence, unpredictability. Whatever the merits of normalization with China in late 1978, that it would take place at the cost of the longstanding and formal commitment made by the United States to the government of Taiwan was bound to be of significance to some of the allies fearful that they, too, in the future, might be sacrificed (even if in a different way) to the necessities of adversary relationships; similarly, the timid support (at best) and hasty abandonment (at worst) of a regime in Iran created by, and initially, at least, for, the United States was likely to be of much import to other regimes whose own political legitimacy was open to similar destabilizing pressures from within.

For Moscow, the military balance of the late 1970s was an asset that had been gained at great cost. For Washington, such a balance was a liability that required some adjustments, to be sure, but none yet that might have immediate consequences for vital U.S. interests. For the Europeans, this new balance might permit ever greater freedom of action to the Soviets, not so much in Europe proper as in areas of crucial importance to the Europeans (that is, Africa). Meanwhile, many in Europe noted, the SALT balances emphasized those systems best capable of reaching the territories of both superpowers, but neglected those targeted on western Europe (the growth of which was said to be especially significant) and constrained the further development of those technologies most readily accessible to the Europeans (the cruise missile, for instance). Rough equivalency, then, had a sure winner in the Soviet Union, an uncertain loser in the United States, and a potential victim in western Europe. While this did not imply the coming submission of Europe to Soviet preferences, more fragmentation of the Atlantic consensus on security interests might some day confirm doubts in Moscow that the alliance still had a unified will for collective action to cope with the political follow-up of this clear Soviet military challenge.

In short, on entering the 1980s, Europe viewed the nuclear fantasies of the 1970s with, at best, the same ambivalence that it had shown during the previous decade. Having for years urged the United States to act with restraint and moderation, Europe was now deploring U.S. apathy and counselling more boldness. It relied on a protector whose credibility it persistently doubted, to deter a threat the nature and direction of which was periodically debated, with the assistance of a poorly understood military technology that was itself based on an ill-defined strategy: entering the 1980s, the Atlantic fantasy consisted of believing that such a state of affairs could endure indefinitely.

NOTES

1. James R. Schlesinger, *Arms Interactions and Arms Control*, The Rand Corporation, P-3881, September 1968, p. 17. Quoted in Desmond Ball, *Déjà Vu: The Return to Counterforce in the Nixon Administration*, California Seminar on Arms Control and Foreign Policy, December 1974.

2. Raymond E. Burrell, *Strategic Nuclear Parity and NATO Defense Doctrine*, National Security Affairs Monograph Series 78-4, July 1978, p. 10.

3. James E. King, Jr., "Collective Defense: The Military Commitment," in *Alliance Policy in the Cold War*, ed. Arnold Wolfers (Baltimore: Johns Hopkins Press, 1959), p. 113.

4. See my *France, de Gaulle, and Europe: The Policy of the Fourth and Fifth Republics Toward the Continent* (Baltimore: Johns Hopkins Press, 1968), p. 34.

5. Quoted in Horst Mendershausen, *Outlook on Western Solidarity: Political Relations in the Atlantic Alliance System*, The Rand Corporation, R-1512-PR, June 1976, p. 16.

6. Quoted in R. B. Manderson-Jones, *The Special Relationship: Anglo-American Relations and Western European Unity, 1947-1956* (New York: Crane, Russak, 1972), p. 21.

7. Lord Moran, *Memoires* (Paris: Laffont, 1966), p. 333. Cited in Alfred Grosser, *Les Occidentaux: Les Etats Unis et l'Europe Depuis la Guerre* (Paris: Fayard, 1978).

8. Quoted in Manderson-Jones, op. cit., p. 23.

9. Alex Werth, *France, 1940-1955* (London: Readers Union, 1955), p. 315. Serfaty, *France, de Gaulle, and Europe*, op. cit., p. 32.

10. Quoted in Grosser, *Les Occidentaux*, op. cit., p. 144.

11. Norman Podhoretz, *Making It* (New York: Random House, 1967), pp. 84-87.

12. Paul Nitze, "Coalition Policy and the Concept of World Order," in *Alliance Policy in the Cold War*, ed. Arnold Wolfers (Baltimore: Johns Hopkins Press, 1959), p. 19.

13. See William W. Kaufmann, *The McNamara Strategy* (New York: Harper & Row, 1964), passim. Also, Ball, *Déjà Vu*, op. cit., pp. 11 ff.

14. Quoted in *Tactical Nuclear Weapons: European Perspectives*, Stockholm International Peace Research Institute (London: Taylor and Francis, 1978), p. 298.

15. Raymond Aron, *The Great Debate: Theories of Nuclear Strategy* (New York: Doubleday, 1965), p. 167.

16. Quoted in Sam Huntington, *The Common Defense* (New York: Columbia University Press, 1961), p. 80.

17. Quoted in Jeffrey Record, with the assistance of Thomas I. Anderson, *U.S. Nuclear Weapons in Europe* (Washington, D.C.: The Brookings Institution, 1974), p. 11.

18. See my "America and Europe in the Seventies: Integration or Disintegration?" *Orbis*, Spring 1973, pp. 95-109.

19. For the Carte Blanche exercise, see Robert E. Osgood, *NATO: The Entangling Alliance* (Chicago: University of Chicago Press, 1962) pp. 126-27. On the "stalemate strategy," see Richard Burt's report in the New York *Times*, "U.S. Doubts Ability to Defend Europe in Conventional War," January 6, 1978.

20. Henry Kissinger, *Nuclear Weapons and Foreign Policy* (New York: Harper & Brothers, 1957), p. 132. Also cited in Ball, *Déjà Vu*, op. cit., p. 31.

21. Ball, *Déjà Vu*, op. cit., p. 30.

22. Quoted in Gerald Freund, *Germany Between Two Worlds* (New York: Harper & Row, 1961), p. 115; and Richard J. Barnet and Marcus G. Raskin, *After 20 Years: The Decline of NATO and the Search for a New Policy in Europe* (New York: Vintage Books, 1966), p. 44.

23. Michel Tatu, "The Devolution of Power: A Dream?" *Foreign Affairs*, July 1975, pp. 668-83.

24. Warner R. Schilling et al., *American Arms and a Changing Europe; Dilemmas of Deterrence and Disarmament* (New York: Columbia University Press, 1973), p. 76.

25. Richard N. Rosecrance, *Defense of the Realm: British Strategy in the Nuclear Epoch* (New York: Columbia University Press, 1968), p. 237.

26. Raymond E. Burrell, *The French Communist Party, Nuclear Weapons and National Defense: Issues of the 1978 Election Campaign*, National Security Affairs Monograph Series 79-2 (January 1979), pp. 13-15.

27. Rosecrance, op. cit., p. 238.

28. Ian Smart, *Future Conditional: The Prospect for Anglo-French Nuclear Cooperation*, Adelphi Papers, no. 78 (London: Institute for Strategic Studies, 1971), pp. 17-22.

29. Geoffrey Kemp, *Nuclear Forces for Medium Powers. Part II and III: Strategic Requirements and Options*, Adelphi Papers, no. 107 (London: International Institute for Strategic Studies, 1974), pp. 3-14. See also Alastair Buchan, *Europe's Futures, Europe's Choices: Models of Western Europe in the 1970s* (New York: Columbia University Press, 1969), pp. 134-37.

30. See Giscard d'Estaing's declaration of February 9, 1978.

31. As stated by Henry Queuille, *New York Times*, March 3, 1949.

32. Mendershausen, op. cit., pp. 51-52.

33. Quoted in King, op. cit., p. 123.

34. The *Military Balance, 1976-77*, and *1977-78* (London: International Institute for Strategic Studies), p. 104 and p. 109 respectively.

35. Colin S. Gray, "The Soviet Military Threat," in *Soviet Dynamics–Political, Economic, Military*, World Affairs Council of Pittsburgh, 17th World Affairs Forum (1978).

36. *The Military Balance, 1977-78*, op. cit., p. 109.

37. Gray, op. cit., pp. 69-70.

38. Paul Nitze, "Deterring our Deterrent," *Foreign Policy*, Winter 1976-77, pp. 195-210. See also Colin Gray, *The Future of Land-Based Missile Forces*, Adelphi Papers, no. 140 (London: International Institute for Strategic Studies, 1977).

3

THE THREATS ELSEWHERE

Economic and monetary relations between the United States and western Europe reflect much more than economic goals and economic consequences. Indeed, they encompass elements of conflict and cooperation often similar to the debates over military doctrines and political commonalities. In Richard Gardner's words, "Money means command over resources and command over resources means power. Through the accumulation of gold and other reserves nations often seek to assure their financial and political independence and put themselves in a position to influence the policies of others."[1]

THE ATLANTIC ECONOMIC COMMUNITY

It is ironic that the most visible and most easily measurable U.S. achievement in Europe should have also proven to be the most fragile and, in the end, the most divisive as well. Writing in the early 1970s, a European observer of the Atlantic scene found it to be "obvious that nothing causes as many strains in contemporary European-American relations as economic problems."[2] What a turn of events: in a previous Cold War era dominated by issues of physical security, broad treatments of the Atlantic partnership, whether "troubled" or not, could be written without paying more than a marginal attention to economic and monetary issues. Now, however, in the era of détente and interdependence, volumes could be published that give questions of physical security marginal attention at most.

I am indebted to Barry Solarz for his valuable research assistance in preparing this chapter.

Yet issues of trade and money, as well as conflicts that accompany them, are not new. As is well known, sharp disagreements over economic policy were especially divisive between the two world wars.[3] The secretary of state during nearly all of the Roosevelt presidency, Cordell Hull, had believed that a liberal world of free trade and multilateral payments arrangements was a necessary, if not a sufficient, foundation for any peaceful international order. Depression, repressive ideologies, and, ultimately, war were all linked by Secretary Hull and his followers to the nationalistic excesses of that period, with its increasing reliance on competitive devaluations, quotas, ever higher tariff walls, and, consequently, a world-wide fragmentation into exclusionary economic blocs. War, Hull was fond of reminding the skeptics, did not break out between the United States and any country with which it had succeeded in negotiating a trade agreement: a few exceptions notwithstanding, such countries had joined together in resisting the Axis. In short, the political and military line-up had followed the economic line-up.[4]

So it was expected to be, then, after World War II: Bretton Woods would give a vital economic base to the postwar politicomilitary order. In monetary and economic matters, too, the lessons learned from the 1930s shaped the outlook of the policy makers in the 1940s: no more freely fluctuating exchange rates leading to competitive and mutually harmful devaluations; no more inadequate supply of international monetary reserves forcing trade restrictions and causing self-induced recessions. Instead, the new age was to be based on the recognition of an internationally shared interest in developing and preserving an open and harmonious system, an interest that remained generally unchallenged in the 1950s, as squabbles over access to markets, foreign penetration of national industries, and access to material remained few in number and limited in scope.[5]

Thus, underlying the Bretton-Woods agreement was an Anglo-American plan (partly the former, but mainly the latter) aimed at achieving currency stability, encouraging currency convertibility, and maximizing free trade. Such objectives, it was optimistically assumed, could be promptly fulfilled following a short period of transition—five years at most—during which the disruptions caused by the war would be settled.

With the benefit of hindsight, this initial optimism is especially surprising insofar as the assessment of Great Britain's ability to regain its status as importer, exporter, broker, banker, and investor is concerned.[6] U.S. insistence on making the renewed convertibility of sterling a precondition to the extension of a $3.75 billion loan to London is a case in point. When sterling became convertible on July 15, 1947, as required by Washington, foreigners jumped at the chance to convert, causing losses to Great Britain amounting to approximately $1 billion worth of gold and dollars in just four weeks, an enormous sum at the time. The collapse of this initial experiment in liberal economics—at once ended with Great Britain's abandonment of convertibility by August 20—

colored the U.S. and European attitudes for many years afterward. It shattered the assumption that the return to economic normalcy could be swift and painless. In the aftermath of the harsh winter of 1946-47—a winter that seemed to put the finishing touch on the war-time devastation of Europe—it confirmed the conclusion that had begun to impose itself on the policy makers in Washington a few weeks earlier. "It is now obvious," Will Clayton wrote Under Secretary Acheson and Secretary Marshall in early May 1947, "that we have greatly underestimated the destruction to the European economy by the war."Recovery, Clayton continued as an introduction to a proposal that was to be developed as the Marshall Plan, could still be achieved. But, Clayton warned, "the U.S. must run this show."[7]

While "running the show," the United States assumed two major roles. On the one hand, it fed Europe with an amount of liquidity that could finance its recovery in the face of balance-of-payments deficits with the rest of the world that totaled $5.8 billion in 1946 and $7.6 billion the following year. Given the insufficiency of the Bretton Woods institutions (modestly funded and, in any case, barely used up to 1956), such international liquidity was created through outright dollar grants (approximately $17 billion to 16 European countries during the period 1948-52) and dollar transfers resulting in U.S. balance-of-payments deficits that averaged $1.5 billion a year (as conventionally measured) between 1950 and 1958.[8] On the other hand, the long-term adjustment of these balances was sought through the encouragement of intra-European trade even at the price of discrimination against the dollar and U.S. goods, a discrimination that, needless to say, was expected to be temporary only. "Economics," as David Calleo has put it, "was subordinated to politics. Trade took direction from the flag."[9] By 1953, only 11 percent of total OEEC imports from the dollar area were free of quantitative restrictions, as compared with over two-thirds of intra-European trade, thereby creating a sharp decline in earlier postwar U.S. trade surpluses—from $10.1 billion in 1947 to $2.6 billion in 1952.[10]

That such dollar outflows should not have been a source of transatlantic tensions in the 1950s reflected the mutual benefits that resulted from the bargain implicitly struck between the United States and western Europe: the former paid for the latter's defense (with the end of the European Recovery Program in 1952, U.S. military expenditures in Europe increased to $1.5 billion a year in 1954-59), while the latter financed the former's balance of payments deficits (during the period 1950-62, EEC reserves of gold and dollars increased by some $17 billion).[11] Thus freed from any balance-of-payments constraint, the United States could pursue whatever policies it considered appropriate, and accept whatever financial burden it deemed necessary, to promote objectives believed to be in the national interest. As Cold War tensions peaked, primacy was placed in Europe on the requirements of physical security against the political and military threats raised by the Soviet Union, and not on the requirements of economic security against a U.S. monetary hegemony whose consequences were perceived by some but dismissed by most. In short, such hegemony—reflected in the United States' willingness and ability to determine and maintain the essential rules by which economic relations among the Atlantic states were to be governed—remained consensual.[12] Or, as B. Jerry Cohen has written, "America's allies acquiesced in a hegemonic system that accorded the United States special privileges to act abroad unilaterally to promote U.S. interests. The United States, in turn, condoned its allies' use of the system to promote their own economic prosperity."[13]

Indeed, the United States' and Europe's economies had much to gain from the Atlantic bargain. Clearly, without a Europe that could soon produce, consume, invest, and trade again at high levels, a prosperous United States striving within a well-operating world economy was not easily conceivable. By 1950, all members of the European Payments Union (EPU) had already regained their prewar productivity level, and by the end of the decade their export-led growth was seen, in the fashionable though somewhat misleading word of the time, as "miraculous."[14] In fact, by 1958, convertibility was at last achieved as the EPU was dismantled at the same time that an ambitious effort aiming at the economic integration of Europe was started.

THE GATHERING CONFLICTS

A more contentious era of transatlantic relations was nevertheless in the making. In lieu of the earlier postwar dollar shortage, a dollar glut now threatened the dollar's convertibility—and, hence, its very credibility.[15] By the end of the 1950s, the excess of U.S. gold holdings over foreign dollar holdings had fallen from $18.1 billion in 1948 to a mere $50 million; and in 1960 the U.S. balance-of-payments deficit ballooned to $3.7 billion, thereby leading to the first serious speculative attack on the dollar, in November of that year. Now the countries of Europe—whose renewed strength was reflected in the organization of the Group of Ten in late 1961—expressed concern over the rapidly growing cost of monetary dependence, measured already in terms of the inflationary potential of a quickly expanding Eurodollar market, as well as in terms of the rising direct foreign investments by U.S.-based corporations. Now, too, the Americans—whose new vulnerability as a debtor country was reflected in a call for the very funding facilities à la Keynes that the postwar White Plan had denied the IMF at Bretton Woods—were asking for an end to discriminatory trade practices that frustrated their efforts to contain and reverse balance-of-payments deficits, seen by the Kennedy administration as a threat second only to the threat of nuclear war.[16]

The U.S. strategy of the early 1960s was to restore payments equilibrium by increasing trade surpluses to compensate for the capital outflows generated by military expenditures and direct foreign investments. Linkages between the costs and the rewards of U.S. leadership were thus made all too obvious.[17] With the Gaullist challenge gaining increasing momentum as the Fifth Republic completed an imperial withdrawal initiated during the previous regime, the United States assumed that a fresh infusion of economic interdependence would serve to strengthen the political and strategic bonds required to face a presumed Soviet threat. "An integrated Western Europe, joined in trading partnership with the United States," Kennedy told Congress, "will further shift the world balance of power to the side of freedom."[18]

Accordingly, the integration of Europe continued to be seen as the logical extension of the Atlantic bargain. In time, an economic union à la EEC would lead to a political union based on the U.S. model of federalism and supranational institutions. Throughout, U.S. policy clung to the notion of a continuing harmony of interests between a strong and united Europe on the one hand and the United States on the other. From within and from without, such a united Europe would oppose communist pressure better than a divided one. This had been a guiding assumption in the early 1950s, and it was still a guiding assumption in the early 1960s. Thus Kennedy's Grand Design built upon earlier policy statements that had found it "difficult," in General Eisenhower's words on July 3, 1951, "to overstate the benefit . . . that would accrue to NATO if the free nations of Europe were truly a unit."[19] An outward-looking European Common Market would emerge as a full partner of the United States, especially following the projected entry of Great Britain into the "new" Europe. Thus, the overall gains coming out of the nascent community (first European, but soon Atlantic) would easily outweigh the temporary consequences of external tariffs, tariffs that in any case were soon to be reviewed if not removed.

In a general sense, the 1962 Trade Expansion Act (TEA) was designed to acknowledge the emerging economic power and competitiveness of the European Economic Community within the atmosphere of East-West détente that followed the missile crisis of November 1962, as well as within the atmosphere of West-West tensions that followed the Atlantic crisis of December 1962–January 1963. A key provision of the TEA called for the removal of all tariffs on those products where combined U.S. and EEC exports amounted to four-fifths of total world exports (excluding trade within the EEC and exports to or from communist countries). Passed by Congress following the failure of the so-called Dillon Round, which had actually attempted to reduce the EEC's external tariffs even before they went into effect, the TEA was expected to help achieve two major U.S. objectives. First, the 80 percent rule would facilitate Great Britain's admission to the EEC, since the list of products covered by such a rule would remain strictly limited without British participation. At the same time, it would allow a significant expansion of U.S. exports, since the 80 percent clause covered most conveniently those very commodities (mainly machinery, railway equipment, automobiles, and organic chemicals) where U.S. ability to compete appeared to be especially strong.[20]

Although often divided, Europe's reaction to the U.S. initiative and Europe's hard and united negotiating stand during the subsequent Kennedy Round indicated that limits were now being set to the previously unchallenged harmony said to exist between trade liberalization and regional economic integration. On the question of agricultural products most particularly, it was clear from the outset that Europe (and France most specifically) and the United States did not have common interests. France had joined the EEC with a view to becoming the main supplier of the partner countries—and especially of West Germany, the largest importer of foodstuffs in the community. Consequently, France insisted on the elaboration and application of a Common Agricultural Policy (CAP) that would permit the substitution of high-cost French agricultural products for lower-cost U.S. products. These, however, represented one-third of total U.S. exports to the Common Market: they could not be displaced without significantly affecting the overall U.S. strategy of lesser payments deficits through larger trade surpluses. But on the question of industrial products, too, the common external tariff of the EEC that was established by the Rome Treaty was on the average higher than the national tariffs that it was to replace (especially as regards West Germany): the community was therefore able to approach negotiations based on reciprocity with a much improved bargaining position, even following the pre-Kennedy Round cuts of early 1962.[21]

Further divergences were much in evidence throughout this initial test of economic strength between the United States and Europe, not the only, but evidently the two major, protagonists of the Kennedy Round. This is not the place to review these divergences. Suffice it to say that, even though tariffs were substantially reduced (about one-third for nonagricultural products in developed countries), these negotiations exposed the boundaries of an integrated transatlantic economy in the rapidly evolving environment of international economic affairs. Yet the Kennedy Round also confirmed, at this late date, the continued U.S. commitment to the principles that had shaped the making of the Bretton Woods system, for, in spite of increasing protectionist pressures from the Congress, the Johnson administration made the concessions required to avoid a trade clash with Europe. Such pressures, however, were all the more manageable by the Johnson administration and the European governments on both sides as the worse was yet to come: the Kennedy Round dealt with the easier part of trade liberalization—tariff cuts—at a time when the overall U.S. balance of trade was still favorable. Much more politically sensitive and technically complex, the next step in these negotiations (the so-called Tokyo Round) would have to cope with nontariff barriers while furthering tariff cuts in those areas that had been left untouched by the Kennedy Round. That in addition such negotiations would have to be undertaken within a framework of serious decline in U.S. trade competitiveness and significant ascendancy in the trade posture of Japan and the developing countries seriously tested the postwar commitment to open and unhampered international trade. In any case, during the years that followed the start of the Kennedy Round negotiations, trade between the Six, and then between the Nine, grew steadily. Meanwhile, the U.S. share of EEC trade diminished no less steadily, until the time when the United States ceased to be western Europe's first trading partner, thereby transforming fundamentally the terms of economic interdependence between the two sides of the Atlantic.[22]

The Atlantic economic partnership, however, was not based on trade creation only. It was also based on the assumption that direct foreign investments would link further the economies of the United States and Europe. Although small in value, U.S. investments in Europe ($637 million in 1950, as compared with $3.5 billion in Canada and $4.5 billion for the balance of the Western Hemisphere) had nevertheless helped with the European economic revival of the 1950s.[23] The Rome Treaty was now expected to pave the way for a massive onslaught of U.S. investment in Europe. Indeed, attracted by the vision of an expanded market generated by the disappearance of internal tariff walls at a time of rapid economic growth, and fearful that such market might be closed by a series of protectionist devices, U.S. direct investments in the EEC increased six times (in terms of their book value) during the ten-year period that followed the establishment of the Common Market.

The various questions raised by such a massive arrival of U.S. corporate investments in equity holdings added to European grievances, as they caused new misgivings over the U.S. connection without, however, affecting to any significant extent its steady development. Starting from the vague premises that U.S. corporations were too big, too mobile, and too American, many in Europe accused the U.S. multinational corporations (MNCs), in no particular order and with no special emphasis, of pre-empting European credit markets to aggrandize their own assets, maneuvering around national credit control policies and national plans, fleeing the surveillance of national banking institutions, distorting both intra-European and transatlantic trade patterns through intracorporate transfers, denying needed tax monies to national authorities by transfer pricing, fueling a politically dangerous inflation, fostering price wars, and disrupting long-standing social relationships; in sum, U.S. MNCs were accused of laying waste the independent ability of European national authorities to conduct an effective macroeconomic policy (thereby affecting national production, employment, prices, and incomes) and creating the objective conditions for political satellization based upon an endemic European technological and managerial dependence on the United States. Thus, by the mid-1960s, many in Europe forcefully argued that, in the long run if not yet, the United States' "free investment imperialism" would constrain Europe's independence and damage its security. "The problem of American investments," wrote Jean Jacques Servan-Schreiber in a widely read book, *The American Challenge*, "is only one special aspect of the problem of power, of the growing displacement of power from Europe to America."[24] The United States' wholesale buying of Europe appeared to be all the more costly to Europe as it was achieved on the basis of an over-valued dollar that permitted cheap seigniorage acquisitions of European assets. In addition, such acquisitions seemed all the more significant and questionable as they embraced many of the newest and most rapidly growing sectors of the European economies—including computers, telecommunications, and nuclear power—thereby raising widespread suspicions that western Europe was facing a dual challenge of political *and* economic dependence. By 1968, U.S. companies were the largest in 11 of 12 major industries—aerospace, automobiles, chemicals, electrical equipment, food machinery, steel, metal products, paper, oil, pharmaceuticals, and textiles—as well as in banking, and the United States had become more of a foreign investor than an exporter of domestically manufactured goods.

What was at stake, then, was truly the ability of the nation-state to control its own economy within an international environment that was turning increasingly unstable and precarious. To lose such control would be tantamount to disarming the state in the face of an ever possible economic agression from abroad. In the 1970s, such fears took on a new urgency. "It is inadmissible," said West Germany's Minister of Commerce Hans Friedrichs in April 1974, "that we should be kept in the dark about sales, policies, prices, and profits of the international petroleum companies, which are operating in our territory and which are behaving like a state within a state."[25] With nearly two-thirds of Europe's oil supply managed by seven companies, five of them U.S. companies, national governments could legitimately expect total cooperation. That doubts would nevertheless be expressed, even by a state like West Germany, whose higher level of domestic prices for the major petroleum products had made it a favorite of the companies, and that conflicts with the MNCs existed even in those cases when the government had a major interest in the oil company most directly involved (as was the case in France where the Compagnie Francaise des Pétroles was 42 percent state-owned) reflected the growing concern over the question of control.[26]

At French insistence, the "challenge" in trade had been met with a reasonably united European will. But as regards the challenge of direct investments, the European response was considerably more fragmented and, in the end, significantly more acquiescent. Often at the vanguard of scientific and technological development, the industries that were most exposed to foreign takeovers were deemed to be all the more vital as they encompassed sectors where the distinction between civilian and military use was at best tenuous.[27] To obstruct U.S. capital thanks to a European framework that might ultimately denationalize such industries just as effectively would therefore prove to be self-defeating in terms of the nationalist objectives used to justify such obstruction in the first place. Accordingly, European governments remained equally reluctant to permit the development of non-Atlantic, intra-European mergers, as each government strove to preserve its own accomplishments in areas of high technology. When pursued, nevertheless, such mergers generally had limited scope, or even an uncertain future in the light of a determined opposition from the United States (as with the Concorde, and for a time at least, the Airbus projects, for example).

Yet, although anxious to go it alone, the countries of Europe could not ignore entirely the numerous advantages that U.S. multinational corporations admittedly offered. Thus, acknowledged and often endorsed by a majority of Europe's elites, there developed a systematic rebuttal of the objections made on economic grounds to U.S. investments. Accordingly, it was pointedly argued that the MNCs could contribute to a significant variety of gains in efficiency and welfare maximization, in external accounts (at least in the short term) and in employment, in broadening the tax base, and in technological and entrepreneurial transfers, thereby leading to a more dynamic and more competitive economic environment for Europe. In addition, an underlying assumption behind the formation of the EEC had been that success was a function of size and that the U.S. model of technological and industrial development was indispensable if Europe was ever again to regain control of its own destiny. Torn between the conflicting pulls of national preferences and transnational necessities, European governments therefore often chose—paradoxically enough—alliances with strong U.S. multinationals as the easiest way to superior technology, Eurodollar financing, and the U.S. market. Not surprisingly then, the size and the scope of U.S. investments in Europe continued to grow, nearly doubling between 1965 ($6.3 billion) and 1970 ($11.7 billion), and steadily increasing thereafter.

CHALLENGES TO THE DOLLAR SYSTEM

The rise of U.S. direct investments, however, was only one aspect of the more general question of the dollar as the kingpin of a monetary system of fixed exchange rates. Started by the French in early 1965, gold conversions were designed to show the unworkability of an internationally created key reserve currency for liquidity: France was returning to the positions that it had argued, to no avail, at Bretton Woods. A new international unit of account was required—a proposition now readily accepted in Washington—but one that would escape the United States' dominant influence at the IMF—a proposition fiercely defended in Paris.[28] That agreement was reached in 1968 over the creation of such new units, the Special Drawing Rights (SDRs), and that their joint management was assumed by the previously formed Group of Ten, within which Europe enjoyed a veto power on the issue, reflected the redistribution of monetary power that had taken place since Bretton Woods.[29]

However, while most European states were willing to share whatever benefits might come out of France's policies, they were not yet ready to condone and pursue many of these policies because of possible U.S. reprisals, reprisals not so much in the monetary field as in broad political and security areas. Thus, in 1967, West Germany explicitly confirmed its opposition to the French offensive against the dollar.[30] The largest recipient of dollar reserves, West Germany was also the main recipient of U.S. troops: to close the door to the arrival of the former might open the door to the departure of the latter, especially at a time when the Mansfield Amendment, which called for such a withdrawal, was making its yearly bids for congressional support. Subsequently, the dramatic weakening of the franc following the tumultous events of May 1968 stalled the French policy and facilitated a renewed U.S. neglect of the issue for the remainder of the Bretton Woods era (1968–71).[31] The fact is that no alternative to the dollar was left, since its two rivals as international reserve assets had been eliminated: the sterling when it effectively merged with the dollar via the Basle Agreements following the sterling crisis and the 14.3 percent sterling devaluation in November 1967; and gold, following the negotiation in March 1968 of a two-tiered market, which froze the further growth of gold reserves in view of the forthcoming creation of SDRs. An unexpected U.S. balance-of-payments surplus in 1969 (due in large part to the domestic credit squeeze that led to massive borrowing abroad by U.S. banks) helped ease further the pressure from Europe.

Such a reprieve did little to reduce the accelerating pace of systemic decline. The increasingly anarchic character of international monetary affairs was mirrored in the flows of "hot" speculative money from one currency to another. The Bretton Woods system had been predicated on the belief that relative exchange rate stability was necessary to maximize the growth of world trade and investment opportunities in a more open world; hence the institution of a par value system that was to keep currency fluctuations within a tight band of plus or minus 1 percent. Although nations were entitled to alter their exchange rates in cases of "fundamental disequilibrium," no major rate adjustments occurred between 1949 (when a sterling crisis touched off a world-wide wave of devaluations) and 1967, with the notable exception of the devaluations of the French franc in 1957 and again in 1958. Despite the persistence of substantial dollar deficits, the United States—the key reserve country and "numéraire" of the system—continued to equate the stability of the system with an unchanging and unchangeable U.S. dollar rate: thus the most effective and efficient adjustment mechanism remained denied to the policy makers in Washington. Instead, as of 1967, an already over-valued dollar actually appreciated in value even as it weakened in credibility in a period of currency transfers and related exchange rates crises that indicated all too clearly a diminishing international confidence in the entire framework of existing exchange rates: the devaluation of the sterling in 1967; the crisis of bearishness on the French franc and bullishness on the German mark in 1968; the devaluation of the French franc in August 1969; and the revaluation of the German mark two months later.

At the December 1969 Hague Summit of the EEC, post-de Gaulle France, fearful of the consequences that such currency instability might have on the delicate structure of the CAP, appeared to be anxious to move forward into a new (monetary) dimension of European integration. To gain West Germany's support, the French government therefore lifted its previous opposition to the immediate resumption of the negotiations over the admission of Great Britain into the Common Market—negotiations that had been effectively stalled since January 1963. Subsequently, the so-called Werner Report of October 1970 described a European Monetary Union (EMU) that might be achieved within ten years. By reducing Europe's dependence on the dollar and by enhancing Europe's monetary power vis-à-vis the United States, the EMU was designed to shield Europe from the destabilizing transmissions of the Eurodollar glut. In short, it might re-establish some European control of monetary conditions in Europe. But even the first modest steps that were agreed upon at the Hague could not be implemented in the midst of the monetary storm that followed the dollar crises of the spring and midsummer of 1971.[32]

Thus, by the early 1970s, the two intersecting axes of Atlantic conflicts in economic and monetary matters could be seen quite clearly. One, within Europe, pitted Paris against Bonn. While both European capitals could theoretically reach an accord over the EMU—"to weaken the undue dependence of the member countries on the dollar"[33]—they could not in practice resolve such fundamental questions as whether the EMU required monetary solidarity before harmonization of economic policy (the French position) or economic harmonization before monetary solidarity (the German position). Accordingly, the Werner Report envisaged integration solely as a process of convergence of existing currencies, a process all the more vague as the report did not lay down any rigid timetable or specify any of the measures to be taken during any but the relatively timid first stage that was to run until the end of 1973.

The Germans were in addition drawn into the other front, which pitted France (occasionally with, occasionally without, the rest of Europe) against Washington. Because of its prior "understandings," Bonn had little choice but to accumulate unwanted dollars in 1970 when the U.S. balance of payments plummeted to a $9.8 billion deficit.[34] However, when the deterioration continued at an extraordinarily faster pace in 1971 (a $29.8 billion deficit), Bonn joined Paris in opposing U.S. complaints over trade discriminations and unequal defense burdens.

There was much truth, of course, in Secretary of the Treasury John Connally's forceful criticism of EEC discrimination against U.S. exports, especially agricultural exports. Such discrimination hampered Washington's efforts to improve its balance of trade and correct its balance of payments.[35] From 1962, when the CAP was first introduced, to 1972, EEC imports of agricultural products subject to the CAP's variable levy had declined by one-third, while total world imports had nearly trebled and total U.S. agricultural exports had increased by over 50 percent.[36] "If we expect to invest freely abroad," warned

Paul Volcker, then undersecretary for monetary affairs, in late 1969, "to provide aid, and to carry our military responsibilities, we must, over time, provide the bulk of the resources through a strong trade and current account position."[37]

But it was no less true, as the EEC was quick to retort, that the Atlantic balance of trade remained eminently favorable to the United States, which had enjoyed a trade surplus with EEC and EFTA countries every year since 1958; that the United States maintained the same average tariffs as the EEC; that U.S. quotas covered 17 percent of its industrial imports, as compared with 4 percent for the EEC; that the U.S. selling price system had not been dismantled; and that the United States maintained preferential buying programs, as well as especially effective antidumping laws.[38]

Such polemics, however, diverted attention from the root causes of the problem—namely, that during the 25 years that followed the end of World War II, the European (and Japanese) economies had become increasingly competitive. Throughout the 1960s, average annual growth rates, growth in output per man hour, share in world exports and in gross world output, as well as other fundamental international economic indicators, all reflected a secular decline in U.S. technological leadership and export competitiveness.[39] Paradoxically, then, the U.S. economy had grown more export-dependent while it had become less competitive, at first because of Europe's initial advantages of backwardness, lower wage scales, and more aggressive managerial policies, later because the development of subsidiaries abroad had diverted important resources away from the expansion and modernization of domestic facilities. Consequently, the share of U.S. exports as a percentage of total domestic production of manufactured goods had increased from 8.8 percent in 1960 to 19.4 percent in 1976, while the U.S. share of world exports had diminished from 18.2 percent in 1960 to 12.1 percent in 1977.[40] Devaluations and controls, aided by cyclical factors, might well produce a temporary trade surplus (which happened in 1973 and again in 1975), but such measures—meant to force other states to compensate for the United States' indigeneous weakness—were bound to provoke retaliation and raise political tensions, as was to be seen during the balance of the 1970s.

Not surprisingly, the 1971 realignment of currencies and the widening of bands of fluctuation proved to be both insufficient and late. While President Nixon was describing the Smithsonian Agreements as "the most significant monetary agreement in the history of the world,"[41] the London *Economist* more realistically foresaw that the only meaningful feature of the agreements was "that it will not last long."[42] In line with Nixon's optimism, the U.S. Treasury optimistically predicted that the new rates (which, all in all, amounted to a 10 percent devaluation of the dollar vis-à-vis the Group of Ten) would produce an $8 billion trade shift; in fact, the trade deficit was over two and a half times as large in 1972 ($7 billion) as in 1971 ($2.7 billion).[43]

The "tunnel" of wider bands (plus or minus 2.25 percent) created at the

Smithsonian allowed for a maximum of 9 percent exchange rate fluctuation between any two European currencies, and appeared to threaten both overall price stability and the smooth operation of the CAP. Launched in April 1972, the European "snake in the tunnel" was therefore designed to restrict the currency fluctuations of its members to half the fluctuations permissible under the Smithsonian agreement. Once more, Europe's objective was to reduce the role of the dollar as an intervention currency: within the narrower bands of the snake, strong and weak European countries were to intervene in each other's monies and clear accounts at the end of each month. But after three months, with half of the initial members already forced out of the snake, the agreement came more to resemble a German deutsche mark zone; and by February 1973, the Smithsonian tunnel itself disappeared as a world of managed floating without a tunnel was finally accepted as unavoidable.

Certainly, conflicting national interests did much to contribute to the demise of the European snake, as inflation-prone France and inflation-worried Germany found it difficult to agree on monetary policy. Under the influence of its then finance minister, Helmut Schmidt, West Germany's policies toward the EEC grew more exacting and more challenging of the French leadership. Given the overall absence of the political will needed to construct a united Europe, Schmidt warned, Germany could no longer be relied upon for endless subsidies of the CAP—"that white elephant" as he called it—or for ever more numerous calls for regional aid.[44] German authorities also reasoned that, in the absence of any true policy coordination, the benefits of German productivity should hardly be spent on behalf of the speculative crises, inflation, and unemployment of others.

French authorities, on the other hand, wanted to maintain full national control over exchange rate policy, as devaluations were perceived, despite the ensuing embarrassment, as an effective method of preserving French competitiveness in export markets and keeping unemployment in check. Such beliefs implied, to the wrath of German authorities, that French economic policy would continue to tolerate more inflation in return for more employment.

British officials also sought to maintain full exchange rate control, as they feared that Great Britain might become a regionally depressed area despite the aid promises that emanated from the EEC, promises that had constituted a strong inducement in the earlier debate in Great Britain over membership in the EEC. Furthermore, domestic political turmoil regarding the anti-European stand of the left wing of the Labour Party compounded the intransigence of the Labour government and contributed to the persistence of tensions between London and its European partners.

In part, the hope that the snake could function nearly automatically and thus alter the role of the dollar, despite the presence of huge amounts of interest-sensitive, speculative capital, reflected a tendency to underestimate the significance and implications of the Eurodollar market. Even though the bulk of

Eurodollars were held by European citizens, the market continued to function in terms of the U.S. currency, as dollar balances were preferred. In other words, the dollar remained the international intervention currency (implying that reserve repayment would be difficult to enact in other currencies, especially when many countries refused to part with their gold stocks) and the most frequently used money for the denomination of contracts. Only U.S. capital markets were still able to absorb the impact of large money flows, provide alternative financial packages for portfolio managers, and assist the Federal Reserve Board in playing the role of world banker.

Circumstances had changed, to be sure, since the Bretton Woods day—those ever elusive circumstances that had dictated first the rise, and next the decline, of the dollar. They had not, however, changed sufficiently to end its dominant role as the major international currency: in the 1970s, the EEC countries (and others as well) would not welcome the dollar as readily as they had in the past, but they could not afford to do without it either—that is, as long as a viable alternative was not provided.

Challenged in the area of trade by the renewed competitiveness of its allies and the new competitiveness of the industrializing countries, and faced with a sudden onslaught of foreign capital (that, in an ironic turn of events, was relying on its own excessive valuation to engage in growing direct investments in the United States), the United States was no longer running the show within the international monetary system, now in a state of anarchy. But, granted that circumstances had shattered the previous consensual commitment to the liberal international economic order of the 1950s and 1960s, who else but the United States could run the show? Policy actions, undertaken gratuitously or deliberately by one country of the Atlantic area, could have such repercussions outside that country as to cause significant economic disruptions abroad. The Atlantic dialogue on economic and monetary matters now grew more bitter as the periodical endorsements of general principles gave way to the individual implementation of specific decisions. In the fall of 1973, however, a new kind of threat—the denial of commodity supply or the extraction of high monopolistic prices (or both)—added to the Atlantic malaise, as it served to emphasize the inequality of economic security not only between the United States and Europe but within Europe as well.

THE CONFLICTS ELSEWHERE

Western Europe's dependence on imports of raw materials is well known.[45] In February 1975, in a communication to the Council of Ministers, the European Commission described such dependence as a "real and serious . . . problem [that] has been consistently growing during the past four decades." This, the same report confirmed, "is a matter of history: the continent became the leading industrial power in the world because it could draw from its own soil the coal, the iron ore, the copper ore, the zinc ore it needed. When it was coming closer to exhaustion of its mineral resources, it was obliged to import the raw materials required for its industry." Today, the Commission concluded, it is "a region engaged in processing raw materials imported from other continents, and re-selling them as finished goods."[46] Thus, since 1970, the share of raw materials in the overall nonoil imports of the EEC has been between 15 and 20 percent, depending on price fluctuations, with a clear majority (58.8 percent in 1975) coming from other industrialized countries, while the developing countries supplied 31.5 percent of their needs.[47] In 1975, Western Europe's import dependence for ferrous and nonferrous metals amounted to 58 and 70 percent respectively (with 65 and 54 percent of these coming from the developing countries), as compared with 35 and 32 percent for the United States.[48] For countries so dependent on raw material imports, there can be no doubt of the vital importance of orderly and stable commodity trade. In sum, in the words of another EEC report, "given both its sources of supply and its outlets the Community depends more than other industrialized countries on the existence of a propitious climate in relations between developing countries and developed countries."[49]

Not surprisingly, then, following the demise of the empires of its member states, the EEC would have liked to emerge as a third force able to mediate the extremes. But such a moderating role proved to be a difficult one to play: unwilling to speak with one Atlantic voice, the EEC was unable to speak with one European voice either, as national perspectives often continued to differ on the so-called North-South issues of the 1970s.

West Germany stood farthest away (in policy) from the developing countries. Already weary at the intra-European level of *dirigistic* multinational institutions, satisfied with the national and international experience of the previous 30 years, with no formal colonial ties to preserve, and having still numerous emotional concerns to manage, West Germany defended an economic order that, it was argued, had worked well for the benefit of all: "It enabled not only the industrialized countries but also the developing countries . . . to achieve growth."[50] The few adjustments that were admittedly needed could be made within the framework of a renewed commitment to the steering principles of the free market, a free hand to the multinationals, and unhindered commodity supplies.

Closest to the positions of the developing countries were the Netherlands and the Scandinavian countries. A small trade-minded country highly dependent on external supplies of raw materials (but less so for energy than its European neighbors), the Netherlands generally endorsed calls for a new international economic order. Accordingly, the Dutch were in favor of such "extreme" demands as indexation and a temporary (one- to two-year) debt moratorium. For its part, the Nordic Council (of which Denmark, Sweden, Norway, Finland, and

Iceland are members) sought "as quickly as possible" an implementation of the integrated program adopted at the fourth meeting of the UN Conference on Trade and Development (UNCTAD), the establishment of a common fund, the further stabilization of export earnings, a sustained and accelerated transfer of resources to poor countries, and, if not a moratorium on debt, at least arrangements to lessen the weight of debt for the poorest countries (hence the decision by Sweden in 1977 to write off its loans to the developing countries).[51]

Between these European extremes, France proved to be usually closer to the Dutch in theory and to the Germans in practice. Thus, the French rhetoric stressed the "irrationality" and "injustice" of an economic order that had distributed its benefits unevenly and that, accordingly, needed now to be restructured in such a way as to permit a better equilibrium of trade, economic activity, currency, and revenues.[52] In practice, however, France and West Germany often saw eye to eye, as they both feared the creation of a common fund on commodities, opposed indexation, ruled out a debt moratorium, supported the additional capitalization of multilateral financial institutions, and dismissed the feasibility of automatic transfers of technology.

The community's claims of decisive actions notwithstanding, its role as a unit therefore remained generally uneven and ineffective. A joint EEC position often implied a member state's refusal to be isolated, followed shortly by an "explanation" negating much of the "joint position."[53] West Germany was a frequent user of such a technique. Thus, at the March 1975 meeting of the UN Industrial Development Organization (UNIDO), held in Lima, Peru, there was only one vote against the final resolution (the United States) but West Germany then added an explanation that all but rejected the resolution. (West Germany, Great Britain, Italy, and Belgium, with three other countries, but not France, abstained.)

France, on the other hand, remained the country most likely and most willing to differ publicly when its EEC partners agreed. In Lima, with votes taken on nine specific paragraphs, only two of these saw France voting in the same manner as the United States and West Germany, which voted identically on all nine paragraphs.[54]

In addition, where the Germans offered explanations, the French often offered contradictions: now against, now for, resolutions that, rhetorical technicalities notwithstanding, have similarly referred to the right of nations to control their resources and either nationalize ("exercise their sovereignty" over) foreign properties or form cartels without facing international retaliation.[55]

Yet the impact of North-South issues on the economic security of Europe need not be overstated. Certainly, in the 1970s, Western Europe was not threatened by mass starvation, as might have been the case after World War II the Nine were now essentially self-sufficient in edible grains (not including feed grains) and in such basic products as potatoes, sugar, all vegetables, dairy products, and meat. Nor was there an explicit threat of industrial collapse as there was in 1945: with the exception of oil (most of which came from the Middle East), in which case the absence of quickly available substitutes and the inadequacy of current stocks (90 days) made the European bargaining position intrinsically weak, Europe's interests were preserved by the very inability of the producers to undertake effective cartel action. Indeed, EEC experts generally saw no meaningful sign of a critically dangerous supply situation developing for any of the raw materials in the near future.[56] In fact, the list of raw materials for which cartel action by developing countries might have been possible and effective scarcely extended beyond bauxite, tin, and perhaps copper and manganese, with a European dependence of 51, 96, 93, and 100 percent respectively.[57] But even in these cases, the prospects of OPEC-like cartels were unlikely to materialize as the conditions which had made the oil cartel possible and successful did not exist. In short, European dependence on external sources of raw materials was not as serious as a reading of the statistics might indicate, except for those political disruptions that, in part, at least, resulted from the manipulation of external economic factors over which western Europe had lost control.

Fuels, of course, were the obvious and vital exception. As its coal-mining industry shrank drastically—with marked economic advantages in the release of manpower and capital to other productive sectors—Europe's dependence on external supplies of energy sources increased dramatically, from 22 percent in 1955 to 65 percent in 1972.[58] In 1976, fuels accounted for 30.7 percent of total imports (as compared with 16.5 percent in 1970), and, in this case, the economic and political costs of supply interruption and price increases were equally and vitally significant. With an EEC oil import bill that was approximately $50 billion a year in 1978 and is growing, a price increase, however minimal, had a multibillion dollar impact that remained substantially more significant in Europe (with the exceptions of Great Britain and Norway, whose North Sea oil sold at OPEC levels) than in the United States. Indeed, Europeans had to take Kissinger's pointed emphasis on the United States' *relative* independence from external economic pressure at face value—and agree with his assumption that "the United States, better than almost any other nation, could survive a period of economic warfare. We can resist confrontation . . . if other nations choose that path. And we can ignore unrealistic proposals and preemptory demands."[59] It was precisely because western Europe could not so easily survive a confrontation with OPEC and others, and because the credibility of (and motivation behind) the U.S. commitment to the economic protection of Europe was questioned, that some European countries found it necessary, especially in time of crisis, to consider even "unrealistic" demands from the oil-producing countries or others. Or, as Claude Cheysson, then the EEC's commissioner in charge of aid and development, put it: "Europe imports 75 per cent of the commodities it consumes, the U.S. only 15 to 17 per cent, including energy. Europe needs to enter into the kind of integrated way with the Third World which the U.S. is not ready to accept."[60]

If Europe opened and closed the 1970s with an apparent determination to question U.S. leadership, it nevertheless, during the middle years of the decade (1974–78), went through a more subdued phase of conciliation. As it dramatically served to emphasize the differences in economic and military power between the United States and Europe, the 1973 Middle East War altered the distribution of economic and political influence within the Atlantic Alliance. In brief, it imposed both a measure of renewed European unity (but under a West German dominance that only the surprising outcome of the March 1978 elections in France began to balance) and a measure of renewed Atlantic cooperation (but under U.S. direction that only the uncertainties over U.S. policies generated during the Carter administration began to erode).

Implicit in the increasing self-assertiveness of Chancellor Schmidt's West Germany was the recognition that economic power (no longer hampered by the debilitating legacy of the past) now made it the dominant state in Europe. Were there still any illusions left in the early 1970s over a forthcoming French challenge to Germany's economic superiority, such illusions were dispelled by the former's inability to withstand the crisis that followed the 1973 partial oil embargo. Such impotence in Paris appeared to be even more glaring following Pompidou's death, as Giscard's presidency, opened the gate to a bitter contest between the remnants of the former Gaullist coalition and a momentarily united left.

In reasserting German power, Schmidt first joined Kissinger in isolating France at the energy conference held in Washington in early 1974, when the EEC united behind German and U.S. positions. Second, while dismissing the CAP as a "massive misguidance of resources," the German chancellor warned Paris that German subsidies might be terminated unless long-awaited reforms were quickly enacted to prevent the costly accumulation of surplus agricultural food products. Significantly enough, the warning was enforced in late 1974, as Bonn momentarily halted the payment of excess CAP price support funds.[61] Finally, Schmidt in effect served notice on the French government to pursue anti-inflationary economic policies because of the adverse effect that French inflation had on the stability of Germany's export markets; in 1977, the stop-and-go economic plans enforced by Prime Minister Barre at a time of high political uncertainty partly reflected Giscard's responsiveness to Schmidt's pressures. But vis-à-vis Great Britain, too, Germany's welcome proved to be conditional. With Great Britain anxious to protect North Sea oil sovereignty and future revenues, Bonn pointedly reminded London of the immediate losses to Great Britain that would result from a decrease in European regional funding. Vis-à-vis both France and Great Britain, the German government now effectively stressed its commitment to reducing EEC expenditures, be it on regional or on agricultural policies.

The economic disruptions that intensified in late 1973 also seemed to presage more cooperative relations between the United States and Europe.

Throughout 1974, in the midst of a global recession where both inflation and unemployment ran high throughout most European states, the necessity for stimulating economic recovery dominated the thinking in France and Germany. Even though inflation in the latter had remained lower than elsewhere in Europe, unemployment had risen to the highest levels of the post-World War II period because export industries could not sell enough goods to recessionary markets. In other words, a decline in foreign demand for imports similarly affected the German economy. The same was even more true in France, which suffered from both high rates of inflation and serious unemployment.

Yet neither Germany nor France alone (and certainly not Great Britain) could initiate a successful reflation of demand in Europe. Not even joint action would help, as export industries could not increase production if foreign markets for export sales did not exist. Together, therefore, the French president and the German chancellor sought the stimulation of the world economy as a whole, and to this end they turned toward the Ford administration. To be sure, the U.S. economy was itself in a state of recession that was characterized by much idle capacity. But thanks to the relatively closed U.S. economy, the U.S. government could successfully increase domestic demand, following which, it was expected, U.S. imports (still small relative to the U.S. GNP but large relative to the output of any one European state) would increase too, thereby providing the initial impetus for German and French exports.

With the major problem in solving Europe's economic problems thus seen as overcoming the conservative and restrictive economic policies enacted by the authorities in Washington in the aftermath of the 1973 oil crisis, the controversies of the previous ten years sharply subsided. The U.S. economy was still in a dominant position in the world economy after all: European statesmen sought U.S. support and leadership as a precondition for a healthier domestic economy and shrewd electoral politics. No other lesson could more decisively help European nations in reappraising their ambitions vis-à-vis the United States and dispel the self-assertive notions of a Gaullist Europe, as these had been entertained earlier in the decade. In effect, Europe, which had fought Kissinger's open offer for an Atlantic charter throughout 1973, now wanted to turn the clock back even further as it requested Washington to follow up on Kennedy's hegemonial principle: "If we are to lead, we must act."

Initially, the Carter administration sought to provide such leadership through the so-called locomotive strategy, by which the stronger economies (the U.S., West German, and Japanese) would pull the weaker European economies along. The strategy failed when, by the end of 1977, it became clear that Washington lacked the leverage needed to persuade either Bonn or Tokyo in taking appropriate inflationary action of their own. Subsequently, the Carter administration's efforts to pursue economic expansion at home while neglecting the fate of the dollar on the international foreign exchange markets backfired when rising inflation rates reached unacceptable levels in the spring of 1978, while the dollar faced a sharp decline that proved to be no less unacceptable in the fall, thereby causing a complete reversal for 1979: austerity to combat inflation, and a stable dollar to avoid international dissension.[62]

Thus, the pre-Carter moment of renewed Atlantic cooperation proved to be of short duration. By the end of the seventies, policy decisions in the economic and monetary areas still reflected the dominance of regional vision (Atlantic vs. European) and national interest (American, German, or French). The western European allies continued to hedge their bets by relying in part on bilateral deals, in part on increased intra-European cooperation—and in part on the United States. Up to a point, then, the very aversion to risk that characterized most European thinking meant, for all practical purposes, that the United States could still exert an inordinate degree of leadership. Nevertheless, Europe's traditional caution was diminishing as the endless fluctuations of the dollar and the lengthy congressional delays on energy legislation furthered Europe's anxieties and fostered, after 1978, a greater willingness to seek European solutions. Thus, in the summer of 1978, a Franco-German proposal for the elaboration of a European Monetary System (EMS) reflected a joint determination to insulate the EEC from the vicissitudes of the dollar's exchange rate. Promptly endorsed by six of the seven other EEC states, and implemented in March 1979, the EMS could not be as readily dismissed as its predecessor, the EMU, even though many of the problems that had prevented monetary union earlier in the decade were still unresolved (including highly divergent inflation rates that were, for example, four times higher in Italy than in West Germany).

Similarly, by the end of the 1970s the ongoing reform of the international monetary system had failed to deal with several of the essential questions that had led to the self-destruction of the Bretton Woods order. To be sure, the institutionalization of a flexible exchange regime, effected by the Franco-American Compromise in November 1975 at Rambouillet and its subsequent legitimization in the Jamaica Agreement in January 1976, appeared to have solved such issues as liquidity levels, adjustment, and symmetry, issues that had plagued the old order. Yet the Jamaica Agreement had largely failed in its efforts to establish specific guidelines for a well-defined managed floating regime, to examine the continued role of national currencies in the global economy, and to address the issues of fundamental resource transfers to the developing countries. With dollar overhang reaching more than $600 billion in 1978, the prospects for "enormous world-wide monetary turbulence," in Chancellor Schmidt's words,[63] were likely to persist for some time into the future.

Despite the increasing resort to economic summitry in the West (in London in 1977, in Bonn in 1978, in Guadeloupe and in Tokyo in 1979), the same old issues continued to disturb the harmonization of transatlantic economic policies. The nuclear age had not only witnessed the dawn of an era in which the state had lost the ability to assure the survival of its citizenry from invading missiles; it had also seen the increasing inability of the state to defend the welfare of its people. While floating rates did afford domestic monetary authorities additional policy autonomy, they could not be regarded as a panacea to the persistence of fundamental economic disequilibria and disturbing transmissions that continued to persist in the post-Jamaican world economy. In the area of trade too, the Tokyo Round reached back to the days of the Kennedy Round (namely, protection of European agriculture, outlets for Japanese exports, and nontariff barriers to trade). Yet, the Tokyo Round revealed the growing difficulties of international trade agreements in an age of rising protectionism caused by the changing pattern of competitive advantage between western Europe, the United States, and the rest of the world. As for direct foreign investments, ironically enough, the United States was now seriously alarmed by the "European challenge" of overvalued European currencies establishing equity interests in key U.S. economic enterprises. In this atmosphere of continued uncertainty and rising protectionism, a world of scarcity promised that divergent economic interests within the Atlantic Alliance would be anything but scarce in the future.

NOTES

1. Richard N. Gardner, *Sterling Dollar Diplomacy: The Origins and the Prospects of Our International Economic Order* (New York: McGraw Hill, 1969), p. xxii.

2. Karl Kaiser, *Europe and the United States. The Future of the Relationship* (Washington, D.C.: Columbia Books, 1973), p. 10.

3. David P. Calleo and Benjamin M. Rowland, *America and the World Political Economy: Dream and National Realities* (Bloomington: Indiana University Press, 1973), p. 59.

4. *The Memoirs of Cordell Hull*, 2 vols. (New York: Macmillan, 1948), 1: 364. Charles S. Maier, "The Politics of Productivity: Foundations of American International Economic Policy after World War II," *International Organization*, Autumn 1977, p. 609.

5. Richard N. Cooper, "Trade Policy Is Foreign Policy," *Foreign Policy*, Winter 1972-73, p. 21.

6. William Diebold, *The United States and the Industrial World: American Foreign Economic Policy in the 1970's* (New York: Praeger, 1972), p. 22.

7. Dean Acheson, *Present at the Creation: My Years at the State Department* (New York: Norton, 1969), p. 231.

8. Joan Edelman Spero, *The Politics of International Economic Relations* (New York: St. Martin's Press, 1977), pp. 34 and 36. Benjamin J. Cohen, *Organizing the World's Money: The Political Economy of International Relations* (New York: Basic Books, 1977), p. 98.

9. Calleo and Rowland, op. cit., p. 43.

10. Robert Solomon, *The International Monetary System, 1945-1976: An Insider's View* (New York: Harper and Row, 1977), p. 19.

11. Walter Salant and Emile Despres, *The United States Balance of Payments in 1968* (Washington: The Brookings Institution, 1963), pp. 23-30. See also Harold van B. Cleveland, *The Atlantic Idea and Its European Rivals* (New York: McGraw Hill, 1966), pp. 72-76.

12. Maier, op. cit., p. 630.

13. Cohen, op. cit., p. 97.

14. Diebold, op. cit., p. 21. See Angus Maddison, *Economic Growth in the West: Comparative Experience in Europe and North America* (New York: Norton, 1964), pp. 25–42.

15. Robert Triffin, *Gold and the Dollar Crisis* (New Haven: Yale University Press, 1960).

16. Arthur M. Schlessinger, Jr., *A Thousand Days: John F. Kennedy in the White House* (Boston: Houghton Mifflin, 1965), pp. 654–55.

17. David Calleo, *The Atlantic Fantasy: The US, NATO, and Europe* (Baltimore: Johns Hopkins Press, 1970), p. 88.

18. Ernest Preey, *Traders and Diplomats* (Washington, D.C.: Brookings Institution, 1970), pp. 285–86.

19. Bela Balassa, *Trade Liberalization Among Industrial Countries: Objectives and Alternatives* (New York: McGraw Hill, 1967), p. 25.

20. Ibid., p. 30. See also Gian Paolo Casadio, *Transatlantic Trade: US-EEC Confrontation in the GATT Negotiations* (Lexington, Mass.: Lexington Books, 1973); and Gerald Meier, *Problems of Trade Policy* (New York: Oxford University Press, 1973).

21. Sidney Dell, *Trade Blocs and Common Market* (New York: Alfred A. Knopf, 1963), pp. 101–5.

22. Calleo, op. cit., p. 93.

23. Calleo and Rowland, op. cit., pp. 167–68.

24. Jean Jacques Servan Schreiber, *The American Challenge* (New York: Avon Books, 1967), p. 52.

25. Quoted in Romano Prodi and Alberto Clo, "Europe," *Daedalus*, Fall 1975, p. 104.

26. Wilfrid L. Kohl, "The United States, Western Europe, and the Energy Problem," *Journal of International Affairs*, Spring/Summer 1976, p. 85.

27. Henry Nau, "A Political Interpretation of the Technology Gap Dispute," *Orbis*, Summer 1971, p. 512.

28. For a discussion of the European position on the Special Drawing Rights see Solomon, op. cit. , pp. 129–31.

29. Spero, op. cit., p. 43.

30. Solomon, op. cit., p. 111.

31. C. Fred Bergsten, *The Dilemmas of the Dollar: The Economics and Politics of United States International Monetary Policy* (New York: New York University Press, 1975), pp. 87–90.

32. Giovanni Magnifico, *European Monetary Unification* (Edinburgh: MacMillan, 1973), p. 201.

33. As stated in the Interim Report of the Werner Commission, *European Community Supplement* 7/1970, p. 15.

34. Leland B. Yeager, *International Monetary Relations: Theory, History, and Policy* (New York: Harper & Row, 1976), p. 568.

35. Solomon, op. cit., p. 181.

36. Cooper, op. cit., p. 23.

37. Paul Volcker, Speech to the Conference of European Institutional Investors, December 3, 1969.

38. See Robert Schaetzel, "Dialogue of the Deaf," *Fortune*, November 1972.

39. Robert Gilpin, *Technology, Growth, and International Competitiveness*, prepared for the Joint Economic Committee, 1975, pp. 5–9.

40. See *International Economic Indicators*, U.S. Department of Commerce, Industry and Trade Administration, vol. 4, no. 3, September 1978.

41. Spero, op. cit., p. 51.

42. *The Economist*, December 25, 1971.

43. Yeager, op. cit., p. 568.

44. Helmut Schmidt, Speech of June 4, 1975; *The Bulletin* (Bonn), July 15, 1975.

45. See my "Conciliation and Confrontation: A Strategy for North-South Negotiations," *Orbis*, Spring 1978, pp. 47-61.

46. Quoted in "The Raw Materials Dossier," Commission of the European Communities, background paper, 1976, p. 46.

47. "The EEC-Third World Trade Picture," *The Courier* (Brussels), no. 45, September-October 1977.

48. Wolfgang Hager, *Europe's Economic Security: Non-Energy Issues in the International Political Economy* (Paris: Atlantic Institute for International Affairs, Atlantic Paper, 1975), passim.

49. "Development and Raw Materials—Problems of the Moment," *Bulletin* of the European Communities, supp. 6/75, p. 12.

50. Hans Dietrich Genscher, Address of September 2, 1975, *The Bulletin*, September 9, 1975.

51. As explained by Ola Ullsten, Sweden's Minister for International Development and Cooperation, Riksdag Debate, May 4, 1977.

52. See Giscard d'Estaing's speech at the Ecole Polytechnique, Paris, on October 28, 1975.

53. Sidney Weintraub, "North-South Dialogue at the United Nations," *International Affairs*, April 1977, pp. 188-201.

54. Ibid., p. 194.

55. Compare, for example, the French votes at Lima on paragraphs 32 and 59 (j), and on paragraphs 47 and 60 (e) of the final resolution.

56. See "Raw Material Supply and the EEC," *European Report*: "Part I: The EEC's Supply Situation in the World Context," no. 142, May 25, 1974; "Part II: The World Price Spiral and EEC Supply," no. 146, June 8, 1974.

57. "The Raw Materials Dossier," op. cit., p. 12; Hager, op. cit., p. 43.

58. Prodi and Clo, op. cit., p. 92.

59. Henry Kissinger, Address before the Fourth Ministerial Meeting of UNCTAD, Nairobi, May 6, 1974.

60. "Cheysson on Record," *European Community*, March-April 1977, p. 16.

61. *The Economist*, October 5, 1974, p. 70. For more on Schmidt's maneuvering, see Robert G. Livingston, "Germany Steps Up," *Foreign Policy*, Spring 1976, pp. 114-130.

62. Robert O. Keohane, "U.S. Foreign Economic Policy Toward Other Advanced Capitalist States," in *Eagle Entangled; U.S. Foreign Policy in a Complex World*, eds. Kenneth Oye et al. (New York: Longman, 1979), p. 107.

63. Helmut Schmidt, quoted in the *Washington Post*, April 20, 1978.

4

THE ENEMY WITHIN?

In July 1945, Admiral Ellery Stone forwarded a lengthy memorandum to Supreme Allied Commander in the Mediterranean Harold Alexander. "Italy," Stone wrote, "is at the parting of the way . . . [It] is fertile [ground] for the growth of an anarchical movement fostered by Moscow to bring Italy within the sphere of Russian influence. Already, there are signs that, if present conditions long continue, Communism will triumph, possibly by force."[1] Expressed at the time of the Potsdam Conference, such concern was not, of course, confined to Italy only: it encompassed the whole of Europe. Nor was it limited to the immediate aftermath of the war: instead, it actually grew with time. Two years later, Under Secretary Robert Lovett asked the director of the office of European affairs, Freeman Matthews, to review U.S. options in the event of a communist take-over in France, with or without a civil war; and ten weeks later, on September 24, the policy planning staff prepared a similar memorandum that dealt with comparable occurrences in Italy.[2]

With such extreme contingencies looming in the background, ideological tensions between the United States and Western Europe have been tied to the participation (1945–47), possible return (1947–48), or projected entry (after 1974) of communist parties (PC) in the governments of France and Italy, most notably, where, throughout the postwar period, the PCs maintained the allegiance of a substantial fraction of the electorate (hardly ever below one-fifth, often over one-fourth). In both countries, as shall be seen, the anticommunist argument was well exploited by the other political parties and their elected spokesmen. Anxious to consolidate the U.S. rejection of their communist adversaries—"out to eradicate Western civilization as we know it," French Foreign Minister Georges Bidault told U.S. Ambassador Caffery on January 28, 1947[3] — to secure ever more political and economic assistance, the noncommunist leadership of Europe thereby helped devise progressively a U.S. policy that fought communist participation in the governments of its Atlantic allies. Such a policy was for all purposes still operative by the end of the 1970s: said Ambassador to Rome Richard Gardner on January 11, 1978, "We have the right to express our point of view, and there should be no doubt what it is: we do not wish Communist parties in Western European governments."[4]

WHEN THE FRENCH COMMUNIST PARTY LEFT POWER

In many ways, the French Communist Party (PCF) is regarded by the non-Communists as an outsider, an alien not only to the French left but also to France: a foreign party among a chauvinistic people, a totalitarian party among an individualistic people, and a proletarian party in a rural and middle-class country. An outsider party, the PCF nevertheless enjoyed in 1945 an appeal that was surprising in view of the party's history during the first 18 months of the war: nearly 30 percent of the votes at the first elections held after VE Day. The following year, the presidential candidacy of the party's secretary general, Maurice Thorez, failed by a few votes and only after intricate parliamentary maneuvering.[5]

Such electoral success grew in part out of the war years when, in the aftermath of Hitler's invasion of the Soviet Union, the PCF had rapidly emerged as a stronghold of the French Resistance. Although grossly excessive, communist claims that 75,000 members of the party had been shot by the occupying forces during the war years were plausible enough to absolve the PCF from its earlier sins.[6] An army, a doctrine, and a church all at once, it offered a program of action based, in appearance at least, on an irresistible faith in the future of France. In contrast to the widespread economic uncertainties of the time, the PCF promised prompt recovery and welfare for all. Throughout the country, the collapse of the traditional leadership of the Third Republic, much of which had been compromised by the Vichy Regime, created opportunities that were readily exploited by the party. Its new national credentials legitimated the PCF as the party of the industrial workers, in competition with the other Marxist party, the Socialist Party, and in opposition to the party of farmers and that of small shopkeepers. For those who were still skeptical, an intelligentsia imbued with a self-proclaimed revolutionary tradition that helped shape a leftist complex of sorts taught otherwise.

If the war years had blunted somewhat the anticommunist instincts of many in France, they had not affected as decisively an anti-Americanism that, generally speaking, reflected the well-known xenophobic tendencies of the country. Such anti-Americanism stood in sharp contrast with the pro-Americanism that prevailed in Italy where could be found a favourable pre-disposition to the United States, one that permitted a considerable influence on the internal politics of Italy as it embodied, in the words of Carlo Levi, "fable and fact, concrete existence and romance, necessity and imagination."[7] France, on the other hand, resisted such influence on all sides of the political spectrum. On the right, the distrust of the United States was intimately connected with other aspects of French nationalism, making suspect all that was not French—traditionally anything British or German; but now that Germany was moribund and Great Britain on the decline, anything American. On the left, the United States was an ideal target as the bulwark of capitalism—the sworn enemy that had "used" the Soviet Union to fight its wars. Everywhere, a shared intellectual disdain of the United States, the intellectual upstart, conveniently dissimulated the all too evident dependence of France. "The Americans are naive, ignorant, and understand nothing," complained the Socialist Vincent Auriol, who was to remain president of the Fourth Republic until January 1954.[8] The attempt to turn the dependence around was not even subtle: Gallic sophistication, French culture, and Auriol's own enlightenment, one presumes, would compensate for U.S. shortcomings and help Washington learn about world leadership.

France's anti-Americanism, however, was not symbolic only, and U.S. politics, before, during, and after the war, repeatedly met with French opposition. Among these were the economic assistance provided to Germany in the 1920s and 1930s; the delayed entry of the United States into both world wars; the maintenance of diplomatic relations with the Vichy regime and the belated recognition of the de Gaulle government; the United States' postwar insistence on standing firm against Soviet pressure, at the risk of war, at a time when a large proportion of the French people would have given up almost everything rather than go to war; and the perceived pro-British and pro-German (as opposed to pro-French) outlook of the U.S. government. There was, in sum, much mistrust of U.S. goals as well as of U.S. reliability: embittered by the humiliation of its defeat, France opposed the growth of American influence with stubborn suspicion and resistance, naturally most in evidence among the French left. Yet this mistrust was self-contained, and there was an "American complex," too. Many of the Frenchmen who disliked the United States and resisted its growing influence, at the same time loved and admired it.

From the start, de Gaulle was anxious to enroll the services of the communists. But while seeking such support, de Gaulle faced a party that remained, even in wartime, an army of liberation determined to gain from the war the prize it sought most: to establish its control throughout France. Any agreement reached between de Gaulle and the PCF was therefore a matter of convenience. With its efforts admittedly limited in time to the duration of the conflict against Germany, each side wanted to secure with the assistance of the other what it might need most in the aftermath of Germany's defeat.

That the PCF expected to seize power in the end is hardly to be doubted. From within, as the only sound political organization left in France, it would be the sole national party capable of ensuring order in the midst of the anarchy that would follow the collapse of Germany and the dismemberment of the Vichy regime. From without, confident of the active support of the Soviet Union, the PCF would provide security against a future revival of German militarism.

Power, then, did not have to be gained by force. In truth, the PCF had neither the inclination nor the ability to do so. Instead, to attain its objectives— "under the cloak of legality," as U.S. Ambassador to Paris Jefferson Caffery saw it in May 1946[9]—the party attempted to build its domestic image further. Its platform became that of a national mission. Maximum effort at work and production at any cost were the basic Communist *leitmotivs*, as they had been in 1936 during the early days of the Popular Front. "I say it frankly," Thorez warned striking miners in July 1945, "it is impossible to approve the smallest strike."[10] Ultimately, however, a PCF-dominated majority of the left would be achieved by promoting fronts and other groupings going as far to the right as the *Mouvement Républicain Populaire* (MRP), as reflected in such party efforts as the aborted merger with the socialists, or the attempts to merge the General Confederation of Labor (CGT), a communist-dominated union, with the Catholic Trade Union Federation (CFTC).

In contrast to the PCF's courting of de Gaulle, the United States wartime opposition to the self-declared leader of France appeared unrealistic in the light of the then-existing alternatives. As the war progressed, the future of the old political parties grew uncertain, and a return to the political instability of the Third Republic was undesirable to all. If a strong man was needed, the Giraud option was a poor choice. The "Kingpin," as Eisenhower reportedly called General Giraud, remained strikingly unsuccessful in winning the allegiance of Frenchmen; accordingly, he himself tended to reduce his own ambitions and intentions even faster than those in Washington who continued to support him. A third force headed by Giraud could not survive long without considerable direct support from the Allies, both during and after the war. Assuming that Washington was willing to provide such support, it still remained doubtful that the French people would acquiesce to such U.S. supervision of their postwar status, especially if it were to imply the continued presence of a U.S. "army of occupation." Subsequently, the scarcity of qualified leadership was increased when the political reckoning that took place under the cover of postwar justice far exceeded de Gaulle's casual estimate of "twelve dozens of traitors, twelve hundred cowards, and twelve thousands of idiots."[11]

In fact, the triangle formed by de Gaulle, the French communists, and the United States was an unstable one. In part, de Gaulle's initial alliance with the Soviet Union aimed at strengthening Communist support at home. But by going to Moscow in late 1944, de Gaulle was also attempting to blackmail Washington into granting him further support, even while testing the boundaries of Soviet support for French positions (over Syria, for example). Hence the following paradox: the more a policy of rapprochement with the Soviet Union succeeded in leading Washington into additional assistance for de Gaulle, the more de Gaulle would be capable of disengaging himself from the support of the communists at home." I would much rather work with the USA than any other country," de Gaulle claimed in May 1945 while telling Ambassador Caffery of his grievances against Washington. "But if I cannot work with you," he warned, "I must work with the Soviets . . . even if in the long run they gobble us too."[12] Throughout, de Gaulle wanted to impose an either-or proposition on the Truman administration. "There are only two real forces in France today, the Communists and I," de Gaulle argued in November 1945. "If the Communists win, France will be a Soviet Republic; if I win, France will stay independent."[13]

Moscow's reading of the situation was, of course, different from de Gaulle's: the Paris-Moscow pact would strengthen the communist position within France while reducing the influence of the United States. The less fear Stalin created, the less Truman was needed. Obviously enough, Germany played a major role in shaping these relations. On the one hand, it tied Moscow and Paris in their common fear of a revival of Germany's militarism. On the other hand, it was a source of tensions between Paris and Washington, which disagreed sharply about Germany's role in the face of a Soviet threat that was perceived differently in each capital. "If we have an economic collapse because we don't get coal the Communists will probably be the gainers," warned Acting Foreign Minister Pierre-Henry Teitgen, upon which the French share of German coal exported from the British and the American zones was reportedly doubled.[14]

De Gaulle (and his successors) used the PCF as a counterweight to the coolness shown by the United States and Great Britain. But de Gaulle also needed and sought an entente with the Communists, the largest single element of the French Resistance, despite the risk that the party might pose at a later stage. By approving its participation in a postwar government of national solidarity, de Gaulle was gaining a reprieve from PCF pressure during which he might strengthen his own leadership both from within and from without. Confident of their ability in the long run to displace de Gaulle and assume full control, the Communists were willing to pay de Gaulle's price in the short run for fear of being isolated. Besides, any Communist action against de Gaulle, especially following the liberation of Paris, might cause an anti-Communist reaction from without; in 1945, as under the Fifth Republic, de Gaulle could indeed take U.S. protection for granted. This was Thorez's own reading of the situation. "With the Americans in France," he later explained, "the revolution would have been annihilated."[15]

Following de Gaulle's withdrawal, the Communist presence in the government seemed increasingly anomalous, and its surgical removal, if and when possible, tempted both the Truman administration and some of the French political parties. The Soviet Union, many pointed out in France, could not provide the credits needed for France's economic recovery; nor would it provide the military assistance required to preserve the empire. Washington, on the other hand, could and would do both. It was rumored that Secretary of the Treasury Fred Vinson had explicitly requested from Leon Blum, that "the Socialists join an anti-

Communist coalition, and so oust the Communists now occupying important posts in the French cabinet." Only then would U.S. assistance reach the "billions of dollars" that had been expected, but not delivered yet.[16]

Regarding the colonies, too, U.S. policy was said to be possibly affected by the ambivalent ideological orientation of a half-left, half-right French government. In Indochina, for instance, Washington on the whole had resisted early intelligence appraisals that urged recognition of Ho Chi Minh's government. Instead, eager not to antagonize Paris, Secretary of State James Byrnes had reversed earlier wartime U.S. policies, as he now denied any U.S. opposition to French claims in the area. Yet the United States also resisted Paris's requests for military support and demanded, for example, that U.S.-made equipment be removed from British aircraft given by the London government to the French for use in Indochina.

More generally, the reliability of the French army altogether could be questioned in view of prevalent Communist influences, influences which were feared by non-Communist parties in Paris as well. Before VE Day, the de Gaulle government had wanted to field an army that could play a major role in the liberation of France and the final defeat and subsequent occupation of Germany. But to the Allies, the revolutionary potential inherent in such an army raised risks of internal disruption far in excess of its expected military contributions: a high proportion of FFI (Home Army) officers, for example, were known Communists. De Gaulle's repeated requests for military aid had therefore been ignored.[17] Two years later, with a minister of defense who was a member of the party, and with a defense department that was being swamped with crypto-Communists or Communist sympathizers, the situation was seen in a dramatically worse light.

Still, in 1946, Washington "tolerated" the PCF as the Truman administration hoped that the Communists could be safely grouped, if not reformed, by the other noncommunist parties. Accordingly, the MRP formed a coalition government with the two major leftist parties following de Gaulle's withdrawal.[18] The MRP openly feared the consequences that a new popular front in France would have on U.S. policies: no less than the seizure of French bases in Asia and the termination of economic assistance, according to General Billotte, then the acting chief of the French Joint Chiefs of Staff, who was said to be relying for such information on his contacts with U.S. military leaders.[19] "The Communists are doing us a . . . service," added Pierre Mendes-France a little later. "Because we have a 'Communist danger,' the Americans are making a tremendous effort to help us. We must keep this indispensable Communist scare."[20] This scare had been well-fed by Blum during his visit to Washington in the spring of 1946. A Marxist, Blum was nevertheless a staunch anti-Communist and an outspoken critic of the Soviet Union. The Truman administration hardly needed to pressure him at all. Thus Blum could state, upon his return, that U.S. assistance was being provided without imposing "explicitly or implicitly, directly or indirectly, any condition of any kind, civilian, military, political or diplomatic.[21]

By early 1947, however, with Greece and Turkey threatened, the Truman administration saw with increased concern the leading position of the Communist parties in France, Belgium, and Italy. If the Communists seized control of Greece, then Turkey would soon fall, followed by Iran. If they seized control of Turkey, Greece would soon fall, followed by Iran. If it were Italy or France that became the prey of Communist subversion, then the area threatened would extend to Greece and Turkey, as well as to the Middle East. In all cases, the Soviet objective was to gain control of the eastern Mediterranean and the Middle East, with these areas serving as springboards to South Asia and Africa. The situation was said to be especially dangerous in France. "With four Communists in the Cabinet," warned Dean Acheson, "one of them Minister of Defense, with Communists controlling the largest trade union and infiltrating government offices, factories and the armed services, with nearly a third of the electorate voting Communist, and with economic conditions worsening, the Russians could pull the plug any time they chose."[22]

Within France, meanwhile, the position of the communists had become difficult too. On March 22, 1947, when military appropriations were voted for Indochina, the Communists abstained. Only the Communist ministers voted for the appropriations, in order to avoid a schism that they still did not want. From within, the Communists faced their own contradictions; the government was following policies that were increasingly incompatible with the party line, and the double game that the party had been playing since the liberation was now coming to an end. As a revolutionary party, it criticized the war in Indochina and supported the demands of the workers. As a government party, it preached the gospel of work and muted its antimilitarist propaganda. At first, the party's support for the government had reflected the overall objective of maintaining a symbolic measure of East-West cooperation. Now, however, it aimed at containing and obstructing U.S. influence in France. Yet the French communists still regarded their position as moderately secure, and Thorez simply assumed that there could not be any government without Communist participation.

Thus the untenability of the Communist position was intimately related to the conditions that prevailed not only abroad but also within the party itself and in France. Assuming, as did Thorez, that there could not be a viable government without Communist participation, de Gaulle, already eager to return to power, asked for their expulsion. This would force a political crisis that, in the general's view, he alone could solve. A Gaullist party was in the making, and its growth was largely predicated on the existence of a Communist threat to the continuity of national institutions. But the Gaullist position in turn further convinced the French prime minister to deal with the communist cancer, since such Gaullist gains would conceivably occur at the expense of the electoral support of the Radical party (and, of course, of the MRP). In May 1947, then,

Communist participation in the French government had become everyone's target—within the party itself (and also in Moscow), within the government, within the opposition, *and* in the United States, where Truman had just declared war on "the totalitarian way of life." Ramadier's decision to expel the Communists was but the implementation of this consensus. Although it met with the support of the United States—"the best that could be hoped for," Caffery cabled Secretary Marshall on May 12, 1947[23] —the decision proper was made in Paris.

As previously indicated, while a legitimate partner in the government, the PCF never lost sight of its ultimate objective: control of the majority to achieve communist goals, at home and abroad. Once out of power, the PCF rapidly adjusted its tactics to fit the requirements of its long-term objectives. Renouncing the opportunism of government participation, the party returned to its revolutionary tradition. Strike agitation escalated from June on. One by one all vital sectors of the economy were affected. As soon as one strike was settled, another commenced, the series leaving behind it the appearance of a concerted effort to challenge governmental authority. "A sort of circular movement of strikes is developing, from sector to sector, as if there were a secret *'chef d'orchestre'*," pointedly noted Ramadier on June 3rd. "It affects, as if by chance, the most sensitive points of our economy."[24]

This, however, was only a timid beginning. Sharply rebuked by the Cominform in late September for its strategy of conciliation, and urged by the Soviets to show greater initiative in combatting U.S. imperialism, the PCF intensified its campaign to discredit and disrupt government policies. Civil order was threatened. "Nothing," Thorez warned in late October, "can be done in France without the Communist Party whose role is only beginning."[25] Condemning the government for pandering to U.S. capitalism, the PCF focused its attacks on the Socialists, whose leaders (Ramadier and Blum) were made responsible for the current situation. So was ended the collaboration with the Socialists that had marked the era of the Popular Front, the National Front, and the early postwar years, to be replaced now with a fierce determination to oppose all bourgeois political forces, including the Gaullists and the Socialists. Throughout the fall, the work stoppage epidemic spread under the guidance of a newly formed national strike committee headed by Communist Union boss, Benoit Frachon: ports, railroads, coal mines, postal services, electricity, textiles, chemicals, and food were paralyzed, and France was virtually shut down. Labor unrest and social disturbances continued well into 1948: striking workers occupied factories and all services were impaired to one degree or another, at one time or another. "I am now certain that French Communist agents received a sum of 100 million francs to wage their campaign of disorganization against our economy," complained Premier Henry Queuille in early October 1948, shortly before the CGT opened its Twenty-seventh Congress by stating that it intended explicitly "to orchestrate and in any case to encourage strike movements,"[26] and as an indefinite coal strike was about to force repeated power blackouts due to shortages of electric power.

Such an account need not be pursued at any length. The point is that the unruly behavior of the PCF after May 1947 at first owed as much to internal political conditions in France as it did to the global battle being waged outside the confines of the country. In the summer, the attempt to discredit the capacity of the government to govern may initially have been intended to forge anew the Socialist-Communist alliance and create conditions for a popular front type of government: Thorez and other high-ranking Communists had grown accustomed to the accoutrements of power, which they expected to regain. But following the Cominform meeting of late September, the subsequent obstruction by the PCF was the result more of external considerations than of the parochial interests of internal politics: a "foreign national party," the PCF ceased to be a legitimate partner in any significant political coalition in France until the negotiation of the *Programme Commun de la Gauche* (Common Program of the Left) in 1972.

WHEN THE ITALIAN COMMUNIST PARTY LEFT POWER

As in France, the Italian Communist Party (PCI) appeared, in the midst of the moral and material ruins left by two decades of fascism and several years of war, as the only sound and coherent political organization in the country. Even more than in France, though, the quality of the PCI's leadership enhanced further the party's ability to reach the people directly and continuously. More reluctant than its French counterpart to implement the wholesale wrecking plans that would be officially urged in 1947 by the Cominform, Palmiro Togliatti proved to be especially skilled in squeezing maximum tactical independence from the directives of Moscow.

As in France, too, the party's record of active underground opposition to fascism, as well as the wartime performance of the partisan movements, added to the party's prestige, while its ideology fitted the national mood of rebirth and utopianism. Thus, it was widely estimated that approximately two-thirds of all the overt partisans had been enrolled in the Garibaldi formations, and although not all of these were Communists, they had been nevertheless subjected to vigorous indoctrination by the party's political commissars.

It follows that, as in France, the workers, especially in the north, were believed to have arms in their hands, and, in the aftermath of the liberation, the Allied Command ordered the demobilization and disarming of partisan units. Even though these orders were only partially carried out, and quantities of weapons may indeed have been hidden away, it remains that, as in France, such fears of a Communist-sponsored armed insurrection were not justified, as the conquest of power by military means remained outside of the PCI's plans.

Finally, as in France, the PCI faced an early political dilemma with the emergence of a "strong man," Ferruccio Parri, whose prestige as an antifascist organizer led to the creation of a government of national unity. In dealing with Parri, the party's position was somewhat similar to that of the French Communists toward de Gaulle: excessive success for the new prime minister might win him the allegiance of the masses whose sole guardian the PCI expected to remain. The Parri experiment, however, collapsed even faster than the de Gaulle experiment (November 24, 1945). Furthermore, during his few months in power, Parri, more than de Gaulle, resisted extensive cooperation with the Communists. As 1945 was coming to an end, the period of wartime (antifacist) solidarity had already ended, and newly formed political groups on the right were denouncing the Resistance as a Communist conspiracy, while nostalgia for the old regime was already being unveiled through such slogans as "one was better off when one was worse off."[27]

From the start (July 1946) De Gasperi's second coalition government lacked stability. From within, deprived of the unifying effect of the fight against fascism, the major groups that were part of the government were little motivated to come to a lasting agreement on any one subject; positions reached privately in cabinet meetings were soon discarded at the council door, as individual ministers often took an opposing position in public for the sake of ideological and tactical gains. From without, as UNRRA (United Nations Relief and Rehabilitation Administration) assistance was scheduled to end shortly, dispatches from Washington regarding future aid added to De Gasperi's bleak perception of Italy's potential for recovery: everything was needed, and little was offered. In sum, from within and from without, pressures were being exerted on the prime minister, who himself was probably in favor of tripartism, to dismantle his coalition at the earliest possible opportunity.[28]

For here, too, the domestic and international settings could not be disassociated. Since the end of the war, Italy's search for security and reconstruction had been tied to its search for international acceptance. Reconstruction could not be achieved without a level of external assistance that was itself dependent on the erosion of the suspicion aroused by Italy's wartime status. In pursuing such objectives, Italy could depend on a special relationship with the United States, where an influential Italo-American lobby demanded that the United States exert a moderating influence on the Allies and provide Italy with the aid it was seeking. But, on security issues, Italy was not dependent on U.S. good will only. It was dependent on Soviet goodwill also, and no one side could be offended without risking a measure of retaliation from the other.

Undoubtedly, it was to examine the conditions and circumstances under which Italy might become a full recipient of the United States' assistance that De Gasperi accepted an invitation to attend an international conference in Cleveland, in early January 1947. Although unofficial, De Gasperi's trip was reminiscent of Blum's; but even more than in the case of his French counterpart the previous year, the Italian prime minister was undertaking a dialogue of unequals. Received in Washington almost as an afterthought—a 30-minute meeting with

President Truman[29]—De Gasperi relied heavily on the Communist threat as his main trump card. Intense political pressure, he pointedly told Secretary Byrnes (himself about to be replaced), was being exerted on the PCI to bring Italy within the orbit of Soviet influence. While the prime minister was, "of course," totally opposed to such action, he needed much support at once, and any delay in extending it might lead to "semi-revolutionary riots and disturbances."[30] Reading from the record of the meeting, it is difficult to say who was using whom. In effect, De Gasperi was telling Byrnes what the Italian ambassador in Washington thought the U.S. secretary wanted to hear. Yet, upon his return to Italy, De Gasperi, like Blum before him, insisted that he had made great efforts to resist the widespread anticommunism he had found in a country that, as Senator Vandenberg had told him, did "not want to waste [its] resources aiding tendencies that are contrary to [its] principles and [its] goal of internal and international democracy."[31]

Thus, upon his return to Rome, with only a small loan and some promises, De Gasperi announced his resignation, giving as reasons for his limited success in Washington the United States' lack of confidence in the stability of the Italian democratic system and adding that without a clarification of party relations such confidence could not be promoted further. "No political conditions have been set by the American government for its help." said De Gasperi to the press.[32] "I dodged," explained the Italian leader, "indiscreet questions and recalled the contributions with blood given by Communists to the struggle of liberation."[33] Yet, clearly enough, the implicit U.S. offer was tempting, and the Italian prime minister was tempted. At the same time, however, De Gasperi himself was implicitly making a tempting offer, and the United States, too, was tempted. Thus, the American Embassy in Rome was cabling hopefully: "A prominent democratic Christian party member told us today that [the] Prime Minister has decided to submit his government's resignation in order to form [a] new government with less pressure from the Communists."[34]

Responding to the United States' perceived interest in a cabinet reshuffle, De Gasperi was also facing strong pressures from within his own party. While he was still in the United States, a majority of the Christian Democrats in parliament had requested a break with the PCI, thereby confirming a position made clear the previous fall, a position that De Gasperi had then opposed and that he continued to oppose, in part at least, at the time of the January crisis.

From February to May 1947 the deterioration of the international setting paralleled the deterioration of the domestic setting, and, as we have seen in the case of France, the State Department grew increasingly concerned. On May 1, in a telegram to Ambassador Dunn, Secretary Marshall asked what political and economic measures could be taken to strengthen democratic, pro-U.S. forces in Italy.[35] The answer from Rome was much to the point and deserves to be quoted at length:

The pity is that there exists all over Italy a real will to work and there could easily be a general confidence in the future if it were not for the political agitation of the Communists and I doubt if there can be any real effective measures taken to improve the situation as long as the Communists participate in the government. The Communist Party would, of course, fight hard against any effort to form a government without its participation but I do not believe it is too late for a government to be formed without their participation and there appears to be a realization that the Communist Party is not really trying to bring about the restoration of economic stability.

In short, Dunn concluded, "if [Italians] had any idea that adoption of Communism in Italy would cut them off from relations with the U.S., I feel sure the vast majority would reject Communist advances."[36] In the meantime, Dunn added a few days later, in an apparent contradiction of his earlier complaint over the "passivity" of U.S. policy, there was little the United States could and should do beyond providing wheat "so as to maintain life and hope."[37] Here again, the American Embassy in Rome and the Italian Embassy in Washington were reporting along parallel lines, as Ambassador Tarchiani was warning the State Department of the possibility that the PCI might become the leading Italian party at the next elections (then scheduled for the fall of 1947), thereby giving the Communists and the Nenni Socialists an absolute majority of the Italian parliament. In case his message was not being understood properly, Tarchiani hinted: "De Gasperi is considering reorganizing his government either through the exclusion of the Communists or through broadening its base, thus diluting Communist influence in the government."[38] Accordingly, support was urged for any action De Gasperi might take to disengage himself from his Socialist-Communist ties. U.S. policy now was that every available source of economic assistance to Italy be utilized, including post-UNRRA relief. But, significantly enough, such aid was to be granted only *after* a new government was established.[39]

In Rome, De Gasperi's own views had also evolved. Increasingly responsive to Tarchiani's analysis, he had moved openly in his support of the U.S. position. Thus, on April 22, 1947, he was reported to be in favor of continued and increased U.S. participation in European and Mediterranean affairs as the way to solve both international disputes and Italian internal problems. A few days later, De Gasperi took another significant step, as he denounced publicly the disloyalty of the Socialists and the Communists, accusing them of refusing him "solidarity within the state administration and in the legislation on public matters,"[40] thereby adding significantly to the difficulty of holding together his coalition government.

The actual May crisis was precipitated by rumors, said to have originated in Washington, over unfavorable reports reaching Rome concerning the progress of an Italian economic mission in the United States. "As a consequence . . . of attacks made by . . . Palmiro Togliatti . . . on the American people generally," it was reported, the Italian mission had seen "few American officials of importance, and even those that did receive him seemed hardly inclined to take him seriously."* The *New York Times* report concluded, "Hopes that Italy had . . . ranging from a settlement of all outstanding financial questions to the concession of a sizable loan, seemed to be receding into the distance."[41] On that same day the minister of the treasury, Campilli, met, at his request, with Henry Tasca to discuss post-UNRRA aid for the remainder of 1947.[42] The reply was clear: "Unless [a] totally new situation developed, [aid] beyond post-UNRRA year [was] unlikely."

There is little question about what kind of "totally new situation" the embassy and the State Department meant. Campilli seemed to interpret Tasca's statement as the basis for a formal U.S. commitment. He therefore spoke of the possibility of forming a government without the Communists, one that "would, of course, be very difficult to form and would have to have something spectacular to offer Italian people in order to make it a success."[43] That Tasca could not, at that time, make any such commitment is obvious. However, once the crisis had been settled and an all-Christian Democratic government (with the help of some independent technicians) had been established, Ambassador Dunn immediately urged "most strongly that our government take whatever steps may be possible to demonstrate our support and readiness to aid in their efforts to save the lira and secure their economy."[44]

In point of fact, the United States did not openly demand that Communists be excluded from the Italian cabinet as a prerequisite to U.S. economic aid. Rather, the Christian Democrats themselves published an excessive list of such demands. It was a shrewd maneuver, one designed to convince the Italian public that Communist exclusion was the only effective way to the U.S. pocketbook. Did De Gasperi, then, exploit the United States' anticommunism? This is likely, as the maneuvering of 1947 seems to show. Was aid tied to a change in government? Communications between Rome and Washington, and the timing of U.S. aid, leave little doubt of it. Was the U.S. stand crucial to the expulsion? Yes, to the extent that it moved De Gasperi to implement an objective that had become increasingly his own since January, and then provided him with the material bounty with which he could pacify the masses.

By January 1947, the question of whether the United States would help in the reconstruction of western Europe had been affirmatively settled. Once this was established, most of the debate centered on how much to intervene,

---

*The reference here is to an article written by Togliatti in *L'Unità* a few days earlier. Entitled "What Idiots They Are," Togliatti's article was a violent diatribe against Sumner Welles specifically, and the U.S. government and populace generally.

not whether to intervene. Interpreting communism as a totalitarian force that bases its advances on continued poverty, and assuming therefore that prosperity would help curb it, the United States relied upon a certain level of dollar diplomacy to fulfill its objectives. As Herbert Feis put it in early 1947, "We are using [our command over the dollar] regularly to do the work done during the war by the Lend Lease program. We are favoring the countries which we trust; using loans to prove our good will to rulers inclined to bargain; encouraging countries that are wavering in their allegiance to our purposes or our interests; denying those we fear."[45] Without the early unifying personality of a de Gaulle, and without the French political traditions, Italy was naturally more sensitive to such pressures than France.

Not surprisingly, therefore, U.S. participation in the domestic politics of a European ally was especially visible in Italy. As elsewhere in Europe, the spread of such influence over Italy's domestic affairs was meant to preserve the newly achieved political status quo against the onslaught of communist opposition. The nature of such opposition has already been examined in the case of France. Although clearly and significantly more moderate, the PCI's strategy took essentially the same form as that of the PCF: the mobilization of the masses through manifestations, strikes, and other forms of political agitation. Although clearly and significantly more open, U.S. support for the new majority took eventually the same form that it did in France: promises of aid relief and threats of aid cutoff.

"We shall continue to give aid to the Italian people who have demonstrated their sincere and abiding faith in the democratic processes for the preservation of their individual liberties and basic rights," stated Secretary Marshall on the occasion of the formation of De Gasperi's new government.[46] The more Washington promised, the more Rome requested; the more Rome dramatized the domestic outlook, the more Washington delivered both rhetorical and financial support. At times, De Gasperi pressured the Americans to pressure him to give him cause to justify his own action. "A failure on the part of his [De Gasperi's] government would bring on . . . without any doubt a government of the extreme left," the Italian prime minister told Ambassador Dunn, while asking for "a grant of 100 million dollars in addition to [the] present Export-Import credit and the placing of the latter at the disposition of the government to cover the deficit in the balance of payments."[47] Needless to say, U.S. policy was highly sensitive to such warnings, and thus responsive to such requests, especially as the next legislative elections were seen as a close and unpredictable contest. "Regarding the re-inclusion of the Communists in the government," the embassy reasserted on August 28, "the disadvantages in such a move far outweighed any advantages which might be gained by sharing even nominally the responsibility of government with them. . . . Bringing them back so soon after having formed a government without them and now sharing responsibility of government with them would certainly add to their prestige in the country and abroad and would be exploited by them to the last degree as evidence of the inability of any Italian Cabinet to govern without them; furthermore, . . . their inclusion in government was no guarantee of their cooperation in a government program as the old tri-partite formula had so clearly evidenced. . . . Recent international incidents plus their defeat on several issues in the Assembly since the present government came to power were tending to weaken the influence and prestige of the PCI in the country which could only be reversed by bringing them back into the government." In sum, "collaboration was impossible since the ultimate aim was so entirely divergent and that any steps to bring them back in at this time appeared gratuitous and unwarranted under present circumstances."[48]

The internal political struggle (not only in Italy but elsewhere in Europe as well) had ceased to be a conflict between political programs: it was now a confrontation between two ways of life, diametrically opposed and radically dominated by external sources. As Ambassador Tarchiani then told acting Secretary of State Robert Lovett, Togliatti's strategy was but one part of a global Soviet strategy that centered on Italy since Greece and Turkey were now under direct U.S. economic and military protection. Tarchiani added that, while he felt sure the PCI could count on Soviet support, he wondered what assistance anti-Communist forces in Italy would obtain.[49]

In the next 25 years (from 1947-48 to 1972-73), the political situation in western Europe crystallized around the two power blocs, the Communists on the one hand, and the remaining political groups on the other. In Italy, the formal links between the Communists and the Socialists (the two parties ran common lists at the legislative elections of April 1948) disappeared, and the distance between the two parties became even more significant after the Christian Democrats' opening to the left legitimated the PSI as a party of the majority in the early 1960s. In France, on the other hand, the non-Communist left rejected Communist support (Mendes-France in 1954, for instance) and, during the latter part of the Fourth Republic, governed on the basis of coalitions sought on the right of the political spectrum. In both countries, the PCs ceased to be legitimate alternatives to the existing majorities. More a political nuisance than an actual threat, the enemy from within the alliance appeared to have been contained.

THE LIMITS OF CONSENSUS

It is likely that continued Communist participation in the French and Italian governments would have raised insurmountable obstacles to the Atlantic developments of the late 1940s. What would have become of Europe then—and what other forms would have been given to the rivalry between the United States and the Soviet Union—is left to the imagination of the reader. Yet the ferocious party battles against the Marshall Plan and NATO, against the various efforts at European unity, and on behalf of most (if not all) Soviet international initiatives set rather strict boundaries to one's imagination: by the early 1970s, a reading of the past, however generous or however revisionist, showed that the Communist parties of western Europe had historically compromised themselves through policies that reflected an aggressive rejection of democratic pluralism and a steady submission to Moscow's international preferences, often at the cost of true national interests. Granted such a legacy, how would the projected return of these parties into their respective national governments 30 years later affect the alliance?

To raise such a question is not to imply the inevitability of such a development. It is, however, to acknowledge that, generally speaking, these parties have now regained in Europe a national legitimacy that they had previously lost; and that, therefore, as legitimate parties of the opposition or even as potential members of new majorities, they may come to exert, or may already exert, an influence on policy that may or will have significant consequences on the future of the alliance (and of Europe). In short, had such influence prevailed in the late 1940s, there would have been no Atlantic Alliance, and a different sort of Europe would have resulted. Should such an influence prevail in the late 1970s will there be any Atlantic Alliance left? And what of Europe?

It is in Italy, of course, that communist strength is especially compelling. It is also there that communist accommodation to the major elements of the nation's foreign policy (including Atlantic security ties and European integration) has been seen by many observers as the evidence of a growing consensus among Italian political parties in this arena.[50]

Such a consensus had previously been singularly lacking. Thus, up to 1956, the PCI behaved as a faithful follower of Moscow's lead.[51] At the time more a conformist than a rebel, Togliatti joined other western European communist movements in their systematic attacks on every single international action undertaken by their respective national governments. Such opposition was, significantly enough, made "an integral and essential part of [the PCI's] struggle to open and build an Italian road to socialism,"[52] and no effort was pursued to identify, however loosely, foreign policy alternatives of any sort other than an entry into the Soviet orbit. Consequently, alignment with the Soviet Union was very close, caused in part by the isolation of the PCI's leadership and by direct Soviet pressure, in part by the PCI's perceived need to provide its clientele with a mythical objective of sorts, and in part by the rigidity of a national and international setting in the midst of which the PCI found little room to maneuver.

During the period 1956-64, the PCI began to seek some autonomy without, however, breaking the Soviet connection (in Giorgio Amendola's words, "polycentrism does not weaken internationalism")[53] and without harming either the party's unity or the followers' faith. To be sure, such efforts in part responded to several international crises that made of the party's identification with Moscow a growing liability: Khrushchev's exposure of Stalin's excesses, the Poznan riots, and the invasion of Hungary, among others. Yet the PCI's criticism of Moscow remained ambivalent: thus, Togliatti's well-known interview for *Nuovo Argomenti* was balanced by the PCI's tacit endorsement of Moscow's actions during the Poznan riots and by the party's wavering during the Hungarian crisis.

This uncertain search for autonomy did not reduce the party's opposition to the nation's foreign policy. For the first time, however, it did entail a search for alternatives, including most conspicuously a so-called Mediterranean policy of active neutrality that, divorced from that of other western countries, would permit Italy to "participate autonomously and actively" in the making of a "great peaceful state" that would extend from the Arab world to central Europe;[54] hence, for example, the party's support of Enrico Mattei's energy policy in the late 1950s.

By 1962–64, however, a third phase opened, in part imposed by the electoral gains of the previous years (a 2.6 percent gain from 1958 to 1963) and in part made possible by the "discovery" of the opportunities raised by the European option. The former resulted in cautious efforts to define and implement an effective domestic strategy, which included a progressive dealignment from the Soviet Union (the PCI's rapprochement with Yugoslavia; refusal to break with China; and sharp criticism of Moscow's action in Czechoslovakia). The latter implied a more qualified criticism of the government's foreign policy, and the elaboration of alternatives, first and foremost in and over Europe. Such opening to the West continued steadily throughout the 1960s and early 1970s. It peaked in August 1975 with Berlinguer's commitment to the continued participation of Italy in the Atlantic Alliance.

However, such evolution of the PCI implies neither its reconciliation with the existing structures of Europe nor its endorsement of the overall objectives and structures of the Atlantic Alliance. With regard to the former, the party's Europeanism is still to be construed as a continuation of its anti-Atlanticism by other means, even if the PCI's attacks against the U.S. hegemony in western Europe are occasionally expanded to include the Soviet hegemony in eastern Europe as well. In a pseudo-Gaullist way, the PCI wants to absolve Europe from its original sin (the East-West division), liberate it from U.S. and Soviet dominance through the eventual abolition of both military alliances, and open it to the southern states, where the PCI hopes to find new opportunities for Italy to develop a more autonomous foreign policy. Such ambitions were well in evidence during the 1971-74 monetary and oil crises, when a sharp criticism of U.S. policies ("the end of a myth and of a system," that was "doomed from the very beginning," wrote PCI economist Eugenio Peggio of the 1971 devaluation of the dollar; and effort to maintain "an inadmissible protectorate over oil-consuming and oil-producing countries," wrote *L'Unita* of the 1974 Washington conference) came together with a sharp rebuttal of the Italian government ("its yield to U.S. arrogance") that contrasted with the PCI's implicit endorsement of French policies and rhetoric: "Once more," it was claimed in *L'Unita* in January 1974, "France positions herself in the role of leader of the European allies to deliver the Community, fallen prey to the ghosts of the crisis, from the American attempt to regain . . . the reins of the whole western economic world. France, no doubt, takes this initiative essentially to defend her interests, but once in a while these interests seem to coincide with those of the Community as a whole."[55]

Nor should the PCI's stated commitment to the Atlantic Alliance be seen too readily as the base upon which an Italian foreign policy consensus can now stand. To be sure, the party's excessive rhetoric of the past has been muted, especially since the advent of the Carter administration. Accepted by the communist press more warmly than any previous U.S. president since the end of World War II, Carter has helped the PCI shape a new and more moderate image of the United States, "a better world than what we believed and led others to believe."[56] The PCI has now uncovered in the much maligned U.S. monolith a split between the so-called old professionals at the State Department and at the Pentagon, and the new team introduced by Carter: the former defend a past which the latter consider to be not only a mistake but also a shame.[57] Consequently, the PCI readily absolves Carter of the responsibility for policies allegedly favored by this new conspiracy of former liberals said to have turned neoconservatives.[58] All in all, an effort is made to explain, or even at times justify, U.S. policies "in an international situation that becomes increasingly less controllable by the traditional poles of power."[59] At long last, the United States has acquired a human face.

Yet, the PCI's policy on NATO still leaves much that is ambiguous. Within the framework of a vague and very long-term contemplation of a European security system free of military alliances and political blocs, the PCI paradoxically endorses the Atlantic Alliance as a defensive alliance meant to preserve interference from the West. Written into the declarations of most (albeit admittedly not all) members of the party leadership remains therefore a primary concern with U.S. intrusion in Italy's domestic affairs, an intrusion that denies the PCI entry in the government and limits the country's autonomy. Regardless of its merits, such a preoccupation with the U.S. threat to Italy's independence stands in sharp contrast with a stubborn reluctance to consider the Soviet Union as a threat to Italy's security and independence as well. Instead, nonmembership in the Warsaw Pact and noninterference in the Soviet Union's Yalta dominion are ruled to be sufficient guarantees against Soviet meddling. For, as stated by Berlinguer, while "whether there is a desire of hegemony on the part of the USSR over the countries allied to it" is arguable, "not a single act reveals any intention of the USSR to move beyond the frontiers fixed at Yalta. . . . Since Italy does not belong to the Warsaw Pact, from that point of view there is absolute certainty that we can proceed along the Italian path to socialism without being conditioned."[60] Or, as Ugo Pecchioli, a member of the party's directorate, hinted: "Brezhnev has never made certain statements whereas Carter . . ."[61]

Accordingly, and its considerable and meaningful adjustments of the past years notwithstanding, the PCI still holds a vision of the world that is usually at variance with alliance positions, and often in accordance with Soviet preferences. The treatment of African issues by the party press is a case in point: while Soviet presence in Africa is explained and praised as the logical outcome of the international solidarity shown by Moscow toward movements of national liberation since the early and difficult years of decolonization,[62] U.S. policies are explained and deplored as the consequence of Washington's continued solidarity with the multinational corporations. Consequently, clashes between the two superpowers are the result of the U.S. efforts to prevent the emergence of an axis that would run from Ethiopia to Angola via Zaire, thereby "cutting the African continent, reinforcing all the progressive regimes, extending Cuban-Soviet areas of influence, and worsening the internal crises of the pro-western regimes."[63]

To be sure, the assumption of monolithism within the PCI may be all the more spurious in the realm of foreign policy as competence to speak on such issues is much more limited than the willingness to address them. Yet, on balance, it appears no less surely that ideology still weighs heavily in shaping the party's foreign policy outlook. This is not to say that communist participation in the government would cause a sudden and dramatic reversal in the positions taken by Italy within the EEC and NATO. It is to say, however, that participation would introduce new doubts and uncertainties which would, undoubtedly, exacerbate further existing divisions and controversies within both the EEC and the alliance. Probably, in the event of a conflict between socialist priorities and EEC rules, the PCI (like the PCF) would give precedence to the former. Possibly, in the event of a conflict between Soviet action and U.S. reaction, the PCI would give the benefit of the doubt to the former too. When western European apprehensions of Soviet power are low, and the western European reading of Soviet intentions moderate, the PCI can confidently be expected to erode the status of U.S. forces in Italy and, more significantly, limit U.S. access to bases and facilities, especially for activities not integrated in NATO—or seen as being not so, regardless of formal status (with regard to possible action in the Middle East, for example). When apprehensions about Soviet power and intentions rise, the PCI can no less confidently be counted upon to raise obstacles to active Italian support for a united NATO response. At all times, the PCI's unreliability remains evident on such matters as joint defense planning (PCI participation in some sensitive NATO committees, for instance) or U.S.-sponsored, burden-sharing initiatives (need for an increase in domestic military expenditures, for example).

In the case of France, too, while it is difficult to uncover "a" foreign policy of the PCF—let alone of "the" left—it is nevertheless easy to uncover numerous causes for concern in the many questions raised by conflicting leftist interpretations, Socialist-Communist, as well as Socialist-Socialist. Thus, Francois Mitterrand has spoken of a "Europe which does not exist." But he has also confirmed that "France must respect [her] commitments" including, one would think, commitments to those very institutions that do not exist. Indeed, the French Socialist leader seemed to be willing even to add further nonexisting levels to this nonexisting edifice when he opened the door to French participation in an integrated European force that is not to the liking of the PCF, or, for that matter, to the liking of some factions of the Socialist party (PS). Similarly, Mitterrand has criticized Giscard's penchant for "Atlantic integration" and called for "more and more substantial" relations with "the main force in Europe," namely the Soviet Union, which is to the liking of the Communists. Yet, in opposition to the PCF, he has rejected the strategy *tous azimuts* (omni directional) since "one's missiles cannot be aimed at one's [U.S.] allies," and he has remained elusive in responding to those members of the PS who see in "Western solidarity" an infinitely more credible deterrent to the "only foreseeable hypothesis . . . a territorial intervention of the Soviet Union in Europe." "France," Mitterrand has pointedly observed, "has not won a war . . . and cannot win one outside of an alliance. . . . The Americans must know that should there be a war we will be loyal allies . . . [even though] not integrated allies." Needless to add, such analysis does not meet with full PCF approval. Finally, Mitterrand has asked, with the PCF, that the African policy of France move away from the so-called "bloody, racist, or fascist" regimes it now tends to support. But on all specific African issues (with the important exception of North Africa) the Socialist leader has, against the PCF, either confirmed the existing policy (Djibouti, for instance) or postponed an answer to an elusive future.[64]

As to PCF adjustments to the foreign policy consensus set by the Gaullist legacy, they come together with a definite and troubling Soviet flavor. So it is, for instance, with the party's endorsement, in May 1977, of the French nuclear deterrent. The PCF's reversal in this case is embellished with touches that conform to Marchais' candid boast that the Communists take nothing back of their past struggles against the *force de frappe: tous les azimuts*, as if to add to, if not replace, the Gaullist targets of deterrence; no first use, as if to comply with Kremlin policy; no anticity strategy, as if to cripple a force still too small to consider any other strategy at all; collegial decision, as if to preempt it altogether, regardless of the targets; and no additional investment in conventional forces at the very time when French military budgets reverse an old trend of decline in this area.[65]

Vis-à-vis Europe too, the PCF's policy adjustments have been hesitant and generally much less convincing than in the case of the PCI. Thus in the party's monthly publication, *Les Cahiers du Communisme*, the twentieth anniversary of the Rome Treaty could still be greeted with the same gloom as its signing had been received by *L'Humanité* in its time: "It is not exaggerated to think that for the workers, peoples and nations concerned the balance sheet of the European Community is one of bankruptcy."[66] Accordingly, even while the PCF supports an idea of Europe, it still rejects whatever content the community takes as Lomé, the enlargement of the EEC, the European Parliament, and the EMS all face vociferous opposition from the PCF, in contrast to the PCI's general endorsement of all of these initiatives. Taken together, the foreign policy of the PCF suffers from too much that is old (going back to the Cold War era) or borrowed (from the Kremlin, from the PCI, and from Gaullism, however contradictory such a mixture may be at times). On most issues it remains, not surprisingly, a foreign Gaullist party as it attempts to force into the Gaullist consensus a Eurocommunist rhetoric and pro-Soviet positions.[67]

HISTORICALLY COMPROMISED?

The return of various Communist parties to national legitimacy, when completed, and, in the case of Italy most clearly, the rise of their electoral appeal, if continued, mean neither the end of the alliance nor the end of Europe. For reasons that vary from country to country, any other assumption, if acted upon, would help make the avoidable unavoidable: parties or coalitions prematurely deemed to be unacceptable would then adopt, by choice or default, policies that would indeed be unacceptable. Instead, the advent of a Communist-sponsored government in western Europe requires a flexibility that can permit amity or enmity depending on the left's ability to act within reasonable boundaries of permissible behavior.

This is not to draw attention away from the serious implications for the United States of Communist participation in the governments of some of its allies in Europe. Legitimate areas of concern first include the military dimensions of national security. Communist participation in the decision-making process of western European governments is likely to erode somewhat whatever remains of the commitments made by these governments to the maintenance of defense establishments that are collectively strong enough to deter the Soviet Union. Thus, although the PCI is less inclined than the PCF to criticize the size of Italy's defense expenditures, it nevertheless objects, mildly but pointedly, to the presence of "foreign" troops and bases on the national territory. Denmark and Norway, the PCI emphasizes, "without evading the Pact's obligations . . . refuse foreign troops and nuclear warheads on their territory in peacetime."[68] How would such arguments affect the nine U.S. bases in Italy, now manned with 12,000 U.S. personnel, not to mention the various homeporting facilities maintained for the U.S. Sixth Fleet? Granted that France is no longer a part of NATO's integrated military command, how would the PCF affect, once in the government, the development and the availability of the French naval forces in the Mediterranean?

In addition, Communist participation in western European governments most probably would indeed undermine the United States' own commitment to collective action in the light of the public's reaction to such a situation. Thus, Berlinguer's ambiguous reference to NATO as a useful shield against possible Soviet interference in Italian affairs, even if accepted at face value, implies a public will in the United States that policy makers may find dangerously lacking in due time. "Mourir pour Berlinguer? Jamais!" (to Die for Berlinguer? Never!): the rallying theme around which policies of disengagement might crystallize is easy to anticipate. Communist participation in NATO governments does throw into question the rationale of the alliance: a defensive pact against Russian expansion, or an ideological anti-Communist coalition as well? Confused further by a perception of heightened hostility and mounting suspicion in and from Europe, the United States might increasingly seek other options and enforce, at last, the perennial agonizing reappraisal.

That such a situation would emerge without the benefit of a public debate over its implications for U.S. interests is likely to reduce further the room left for U.S. flexibility. A public that has been told repeatedly of the unacceptability of Communist participation in the government of any U.S. ally in Europe would, not surprisingly, find this participation unacceptable.

Furthermore, a major U.S. concern has traditionally been to maintain a satisfactory balance of military strength and contributions, especially with re- gard to the relationship between West Germany and the other NATO allies in western Europe. In 1979, the debate in France over the public election of a European Parliament shows that such concern is still very much alive, as also indicated the year before by Giscard d'Estaing's forceful opposition to any "direct or indirect nuclear armament of Germany," not to mention Giscard's explicit warning against Germany's superiority in the area of conventional forces—which would enable Bonn to make "all essential decisions in time of crisis."[69] Increasingly isolated in an ideologically hostile European community, West Germany, too, might reconsider its overall international posture in a way that would prove to be destabilizing for reasons that remain historically too easy to remember.

The advent of a "Eurocommunist" government may have implications for the socioeconomic dimensions of security as well: the preservation and con- tinued prosperity of the free enterprise system requires a cooperation that would be complicated by the presence of Marxist ministers in positions to in- fluence the course of trade and other negotiations. For one thing, an unques- tionable measure of opposition to the free flow of capital (out of the country) and the right of foreign multinational corporations to select their own op- portunities for investment can be taken for granted. Strict controls, the left often insists, must be enforced to insure that these investments are channeled into socially useful directions. The questions raised by the PCF at its twenty- first party congress are more than rhetorical: "How can the purchasing power of the working class be increased if the cartels of foreign trusts or supranational organisms regulate prices and dictate to France its import and export policies? How can employment be guaranteed if the survival or the development of French enterprises is conditioned upon international agreements which do not correspond to the true economic interests of the country?" That similar questions have been raised by other groups (the Gaullists in the 1960s, for example) need not distract us from the further weight that Communist parties in power would place on these questions.

In addition, beyond the possibility (probability in France) of an outright nationalization of U.S.-owned firms, there is the probability (possibility in Italy) of a reduction of profit margins through higher wages and welfare costs (as written in the PS economic programs that were released in early 1978), and a loss of management control through a variety of worker-participation schemes. Finally, leftist governments may be more inclined to diversify their trading relationships and, possibly, redirect their economies to a greater extent toward the East. No less importantly, they might also be more willing to seek options to the south, thereby isolating further Bonn and Washington on the more extreme side of the North-South spectrum—even if, of late, the PCI's commitment to a new international economic order has been moderated, while that of the PCF appears to be geared more to the requirements of intraleft competition than to those of North-South relations.[70]

There is, lastly, the moral and ideological dimension of national security. In a world of advancing complexity, competition, and interdependence, U.S. values have already been increasingly challenged, and solidarity with those few remaining states that have a common heritage, common ideals, and a common way of life takes on ever more importance. Continued intimate relationships with the industrial democracies of western Europe (and Japan as well) are not mere alliances of convenience. They also reflect a deep commitment to the defense of basic and inalienable values. What role can Communist parties play in defense of such values? However changed they may otherwise be, all Communist parties in Western Europe still subscribe to Leninist principles and dogmas that remain the antithesis of democratic parties. The leadership itself, and not only the party's rank and file, still needs to move in directions that would put an end to the existing doctrine of democratic centralism. Only then would the stated conversion to pluralism and alternance have a credibility that, however differently from party to party, is nevertheless still questionable at this time. Otherwise, if circumstances became difficult enough, these parties might find it convenient to revert to their old ways. "It would take Stalin to put order into the Fiumicino airport alone": brought to legitimacy in the name of efficiency, such leadership might soon reveal its impotence, outlive its usefulness, and still refuse to go.

At the very least, then, as the 1970s come to an end, such misgivings justify U.S. policy that still does not favor Communist participation in the government of any one of its European allies. The questions are too many and too specific; the answers too few and too uncertain. Yet such opposition at this time is probably even less determining than it had been in 1947, when, as we have seen, the existing majorities often used the United States to justify decisions that they had already made independently of U.S. preferences. But to define what U.S. policies should be if the PCI or the PCF were ever to enter the Italian or French government remains premature on two accounts. For one, such policies would have to depend on behavior that is no longer fully predictable, one way or the other. To fall therefore into a pattern of automatic and systematic opposition to the left in power would help the left justify its failures in terms of an external interference that might possibly enhance even further its domestic appeal. The right used the United States to stay in power in the 1950s; the U.S. would now be used no less blatantly by the left to stay in power in the 1980s.

Moreover, the near panic that accompanied the revolution in Portugal, Franco's death in Spain, Giscard's eroding majority in France, and the PCI's upsurge after the 1974 referendum on divorce in Italy has naturally diminished following the mediocre showings of the PCs in the most recent legislative elections held in all of these countries. Even in Italy, the elections of June 1979 appeared to show that the electoral growth of the PCI may now have ended even if the country remains difficult to govern without communist support. In an ironic reversal of events, then, by 1979 the enemy within the alliance is not so much a more or less revolutionary left that appears to be as removed from power as it has been throughout the previous 30 years. It may instead be a more or less conservative right whose challenge to the U.S. leadership, organized from Paris and Bonn, is gaining a new momentum to which we must now turn.

NOTES

1. Memorandum cited in Daniel Ellwood, *L'Alleato Nemico, la Politica dell' Occupazione Anglo-Americana in Italia 1943-1946* (Milan: Feltrinelli, 1977), pp. 147-48.

2. *Foreign Relations of the United States*, 1947, vol. 3, pp. 717-22 and 977-81, respectively. Hereafter cited as *FRUS*.

3. Ibid., p. 689.

4. Ambassador Gardner's interview with Mauro Lucentini, *Epoca*, January 11, 1978.

5. A shorter version of this section, entitled "The United States and the Communist Parties in France and Italy, 1945-1947," appears in *Studies in Comparative Communism*, Spring/Summer 1975, pp. 123-46.

6. At the Nuremberg trials the *total* number of Frenchmen shot under the German occupation was reported by the French government to have been under 30,000.

7. Carlo Levi, "Italy's Myth of America," *Life*, July 7, 1947, p. 84. Quoted and discussed in Ernest E. Rossi, "The United States and the 1948 Italian Elections," Ph.D. dissertation (University of Pittsburgh, 1955), pp. 57 ff.

8. Vincent Auriol, *Mon Septennat, 1947-1954* (Paris: Gallimard, 1970). Quoted in Alfred Grosser, *Les Occidentaux* (Paris: Fayard, 1978), p. 139.

9. *FRUS*, 1946, vol. 5, pp. 439–49.

10. Alfred J. Rieber, *Stalin and the French Communist Party* (New York: Columbia University Press, 1962), p. 231.

11. Quoted in Jacques Fauvet, *La Quatrième République* (Paris: Fayard, 1960), pp. 34–35.

12. Quoted in Steven P. Sapp, "The United States, France and the Cold War: Jefferson Caffery and American-French Relations, 1944–1949," Ph.D. dissertation (Kent State University, 1978), p. 70.

13. Ibid., p. 99.

14. *FRUS*, 1947, vol. 2, pp. 400–1. See also F. Roy Willis, *France, Germany and the New Europe, 1945–1967* (New York: Oxford University Press, 1968), p. 19.

15. Georgette Elgey, *La République des Illusions, I. 1945–1951* (Paris: Fayard, 1965), p. 23.

16. Jean Davidson, *Correspondant à Washington: ce que je n'ai jamais câblé* (Paris: Editions du Seuil, 1954), pp. 15–16; Alexander Werth, *France, 1940–1955* (London: Robert Hale, 1956), p. 314.

17. Rieber, op. cit., p. 133.

18. Simon Serfaty, *France, de Gaulle and Europe* (Baltimore: Johns Hopkins University Press, 1968), p. 30. "It is not to a socialist-communist government that the United States will consent to loan the money we need," warned Pierre- Henry Teitgen. See Jacques Fauvet, *La Quatrième République*, op. cit., p. 75.

19. Elgey, op. cit., p. 103.

20. Werth, op. cit., p. 351. Side by side with Communist actions there was therefore what Alfred Grosser has called the "passive influence" of the party. Such passive influence could take several forms, only one of which is of the blackmail variety. In other situations the Communists would also force implicitly the position of the other parties (if "they" are for, "we" must be against; or if "they" are for, "we" must be for also, so that they do not acquire a monopoly of liberalism). See Grosser, *La Politique Extérieure de la Cinquième République* (Paris: Editions du Seuil, 1965).

21. Blum's statement has become a fixture of any account of his visit to Washington. It is quoted, for example, in Grosser, op. cit., p. 217; Elgey, op. cit., p. 140; and Werth, op. cit., pp. 315–316.

22. Joseph Jones, *The Fifteen Weeks* (New York: Viking Press, 1955), p. 140.

23. *FRUS*, 1947, vol. 3, op. cit., p. 709.

24. *Année Politique, 1948* (Paris: Fayard, 1949), pp. 182–3.

25. Ibid., p. 192.

26. *Année Politique, 1948* (Paris: Fayard, 1949), pp. 182–3.

27. See H. Stuart Hughes, *The U.S. and Italy* (Cambridge, Mass.: Harvard University Press, 1968), pp. 130–40.

28. On De Gasperi's own position, see, for example, Norman Kogan, *A Political History of Postwar Italy* (New York: Praeger, 1966), p. 34. Another version of this section appears in my "1947: The Year of Decision," in *The Italian Communist Party: Yesterday, Today—and Tomorrow*, eds. Lawrence Gray and Simon Serfaty (Westport, Conn.: Greenwood Press, forthcoming).

29. See Alberto Tarchiani, *America-Italia, Le Dieci Giornate di De Gasperi Nelgi Stati Uniti* (Milan: Rizzoli, 1947). Ambassador Tarchiani notes De Gasperi's concern when he learned that neither Secretary Byrnes nor Under Secretary Acheson would be on hand to greet him at the airport. President Truman did not recall his meeting with De Gasperi in his own *Memoirs*.

30. *FRUS*, 1947, vol. 3, op. cit., p. 839.

31. Tarchiani, op. cit., p. 46.

32. *New York Times*, January 9, 1947, p. 7.

33. As reported in the *Messaggero*. Telegram from the Embassy in Rome to the Department of State, No. 176, January 23, 1947.

34. Telegram from the Embassy in Rome to the Department of State, No. 158, January 21, 1947.

35. *FRUS*, 1947, vol. 3, op. cit., p. 889.

36. Ibid., pp. 890–91.

37. Ibid., pp. 896–97.

38. Ibid., pp. 904–8.

39. Ibid., pp. 909–10.

40. Giuseppe Mammarella, *Italy After Fascism, 1943-1965* (Notre Dame: University of Notre Dame Press, 1966), p. 145.

41. *New York Times*, May 28, 1947, p. 5.

42. Sent by Secretary of the Treasury Morgenthau, Tasca exercised a considerable influence, especially on economic and financial matters, both within the embassy and with the Italian government.

43. Telegram from the Embassy in Rome to the Department of State, no. 1328, May 28, 1947.

44. Telegram from the Embassy in Rome to the Department of State, No. 1364, June 1, 1947.

45. Herbert Feis, "Diplomacy of the Dollar," *Atlantic Monthly*, vol. 179, January 1947, p. 26.

46. *Department of State Bulletin*, vol. 16, no. 415, June 15, 1947, p. 1160.

47. Telegram from the Embassy in Rome to the Department of State, no. 1816, July 3, 1947.

48. Telegram from the Embassy in Rome to the Department of State, no. 1540, August 28, 1947.

49. *FRUS*, 1947, vol. 3, p. 970.

50. Robert Putnam, "Italian Foreign Policy: The Emerging Consensus," in *Italy at the Polls*, ed. Howard R. Penniman (Washington, D.C.: American Enterprise Institute, 1977), pp. 287–326.

51. Donald Blackmer, *Unity in Diversity* (Cambridge, Mass.: M.I.T. Press, 1968).

52. Quoted in F. Roy Willis, *Italy Chooses Europe* (New York: Oxford University Press, 1971), p. 291. See also Severino Galante, *La Politica del PCI e il Patto Atlantico* (Padova: Marsilio, 1973).

53. Quoted in A. Dallin, ed., *Diversity in International Communism* (New York: Columbia University Press, 1963), p. 432.

54. Sergio Segre, "Italia Atlantica o Mediterranea," *Rinascita*, 1957, no. 12, p. 588. See also R. Mieli, "L'Italia nel Mediterraneo: Un Assenza ingiustificata," *Rinascita*, 1957, no. 6, pp. 275–76. For a more detailed discussion of the PCI's policy toward Europe, see my "The PCI and Europe: Historically Compromised?" *Atlantic Community Quarterly*, Fall 1977, pp. 275–87.

55. See respectively *L'Unita*, August 16, 1971; February 5, 1974; August 21, 1971; and January 16, 1974.

56. L. Paggi, "Inchiesta Sugli Stati Uniti," *Rinascita*, December 22, 1978, pp. 50–51.

57. "Novita per l'America Latina," *Rinascita*, July 1, 1977, p. 26.

58. L. Safir, "Dietro Carter, l'Ombra di Kissinger," *Rinascita*, January 27, 1978, p. 4.

59. See, for example, A. Jacoviello, "Le Incertesse di Jimmy Carter e il Vertice della Guadalupa," *L'Unita*, January 9, 1979.

60. This translation of the well-known Berlinguer interview in 1976 is provided by Robert Putnam, "Interdependence and the Italian Communists," *International Organization*, Spring 1978, pp. 307–8. See also *Corriere della Sera*, June 15, 1976. For a further discussion of Berlinguer's statements on NATO, see Michael Harrison, "Security Perspectives

of the Left in France and Italy," an unpublished paper presented at the Lehrman Institute, New York, May 9, 1979.

61. Ugo Pecchioli, *L'Espresso*, March 26, 1978.

62. Giancarlo Pajetta, "La Distensione alla Prova," *Rinascita*, June 23, 1978, p. 25; Romano Ledda, "Il Secondo Risveglio Africano," *Rinascita*, April 22, 1977, p. 16.

63. Yves Benot, "Chi Tiene le Chiavi dell' Africa Australe?" *Rinascita*, September 29, 1978, p. 38; A. Pancaldi, "Nuova Grandeur? Forse, Ma in Cono Terzi," *Rinascita*, June 9, 1978, p. 23.

64. For Mitterrand's statements, see *Le Monde*, January 10, and 16, 1978, and February 24, 1978.

65. Raymond A. Burrell, *The French Communist Party, Nuclear Weapons, and National Defense: Issues of the 1978 Election Campaign*, National Security Affairs Monograph Series, 79-2, January 1979.

66. Quoted by William Friend, "The French Left and Europe," in *The Foreign Policies of the French Left*, ed. Simon Serfaty (Boulder, Col.: Westview Press, 1979).

67. Ibid. See also, in the same volume, Michael Harrison's essay, "The Socialist Party, the Union of the Left, and French National Security."

68. Arrigo Boldrini and A. D'Alessio, *Esercito e Politica in Italia* (Rome: Editori Uniti, 1974), pp. 39-40.

69. Giscard d'Estaing, Interview of February 9, 1978.

70. On the PCI, see for example, P. Forcellini, "Troppi Interessi Imperiali per un Mundo che Cambia," *Rinascita*, June 10, 1977; and A. Pilati, "Italian Political Parties and the International Scene," *Lo Spettatore Internazionale*, October-December, 1977, esp. pp. 294-96. On the PCF, see Ron Tiersky, "The French Left and the Third World," in *The Foreign Policies of the French Left*, op. cit.

5

AFTER THIRTY YEARS

The unexpected and odd detours of history are conveniently bypassed by the leaps of the historian, who can explain away the past through the short cuts of intellectual constructs. Not surprisingly, then, analysts can deal with a past as an introduction to the future more comfortably than they can present the future as a projection of the present. About Europe, even if they did not come to pass, the euphoric forecasts of the 1960s were justified in their days: "In the not so new world that is re-emerging from the liquidation of two world wars and several global empires," wrote George Liska in 1964, "Western Europe now faces the more pressing task of acting as a unity toward the outside, even before she constitutes an integrated unity within, and of acting externally as a power even while she is only being constituted as an institution and an idea." Liska ended his "exhortation from virtual exile" with a warning: "Opportunities, if they are passed up, tend to pass away; and . . . smiling fortune, if ignored, spurns in return."[1] As the 1970s moved on, such a euphoric mood has often been replaced with gloom, as seen through the lament, in 1979, of another "transplanted European" who mourns a "great idea that has been tamed, leashed, and co-opted" by a generation of administrators that compared poorly to the prior generation of apostles.[2]

The reasonable predictions that never came to pass, the compelling warnings or promising hopes that never came to be, inhabit the recollections of one's own readings. For instance, one remembers, pell-mell, Roy Prosterman's concern that by 1980 as many as 40 nations could possess nuclear weapons; Robert Hunter's hope that, by the end of the 1970s, war would no longer be possible; Ed Stillman's forecast that by 1983 the French economy would be the most powerful in Europe in terms of total output; Herman Kahn's prediction that by the end of the 1970s Japan would be a superpower; and much more.[3]

More than most, the Atlantic Alliance has been called names: a cracked alliance, said Louis Halle; a troubled partnership, according to Henry Kissinger; a fantasy, for David Calleo; a relationship of bad faith, for Irving Kristol; a complex imbalance, for Robert Pfaltzgraff; an unhinged alliance, for Robert Shaetzel.[4] More than any other contemporary group of states, the future of the alliance has been questioned, while alternative models were devised: looking for the future that is crouching in the present has proven to be irresistible although not easy. Devised to sort political and economic alternatives, these scenarios were meant primarily to define directions—points of arrival seen as the logical end products of a multitude of imaginable points of departure. But their actual relevance to the future remained fortuitous, as hardly ever was any attempt made to describe the cluster of economic, political, military, and social circumstances that might promote one outcome over another.[5]

Beyond the numerous labels and endless variations, six possible futures for Europe (and its relations with the United States) were foreseen by a variety of academic experts who addressed themselves to the question before the 1973 oil crisis.[6] "Evolutionary" or "status quo" Europe referred to a passive Europe muddling through the problems of the present but paying little attention to the possibilities of the future. Neither anxious to launch a *relance européene* nor willing to engage in an Atlantic challenge, this was to be, by definition, a Europe of transition as it evolved toward something else, with either more or less integration, Atlantic or European. On one side of this evolutionary spectrum, "Atlantic Europe" meant Europe's submission to a compelling combination of security concerns and industrial dependence. Less suspect than others, the United States would be maintained (or restored)—though without enthusiasm— as the natural leader of Europe. An Atlantic Europe meant the abandonment by European states of any pretense of independence and spelled therefore their acceptance of U.S. dominance in fulfilling interests deemed to be irreversibly linked. Conversely, *l'Europe des états* was to be a powerful and confident Europe that aspired to an independent role in world affairs. Focused on the nation-state and with no strong collective institution, such a Europe would be bound by a series of common attitudes on major issues. Most particularly, *l'Europe des états* would want to deny the United States the last word in politicomilitary operations, as well as contain its economic penetration. It would abandon NATO, rely on national deterrents, and seek the entry of eastern European states into its midst. A fourth scenario—that of a "fragmented" or a "bargained" Europe—similarly focused on the nation-state. With even less confidence in institutional cooperation between governments than *l'Europe des états*, a fragmented Europe would simultaneously abandon both the European idea and the Atlantic design. It would engage in separate, bilateral deals and would dangerously open itself to the possibility of being "bargained" away to further Soviet influence for some, further U.S. influence for others. Fifth, "partnership Europe" foresaw a federal Europe in which the member states progressively surrendered their power in major areas of economic, monetary, defense, and foreign policies. Federal Europe was to maintain its partnership with the United States. Its very unity, however, would help make it an equal of the United States. Finally, "independent federal Europe" combined the independent orientation of *l'Europe des états* and the federal structure of partnership Europe. A "Europe tous azimuts" without preferred allies or enemies, it would mark the end of the Atlantic connection. The table on page 106 summarizes various possibilities for Europe.

Looking toward the 1980s, new realistic scenarios now appear to be left. As could have been expected, Bloomfield's and Schilling's status quo models have been overtaken by events: Can the observer assume that the Atlantic landscape that prevails today will remain unchanged over the next 20, or even over the next 10, years? Is it possible to project for the end of the century a continuation of the existing Atlantic debates over the nature of the Soviet threat and the credibility of U.S. guarantees? Is it possible to predict a similar measure of economic satisfaction, however interrupted by recurring, short-lived crises that originate within the West or in the South? Is it possible to foresee a sense of political stability, vainly threatened by periodical phases of leftist ascendancy and alleged cultural malaise? The future may well have an air of déjà vu. This, however, may prove to result less from the survival of the present into the years ahead than from a revival of years long gone. The century, in other words, dangerously threatens to end in the same way that it started: shattered by a state whose military ascendancy wanted global recognition, against a policing nation whose failure to win a war at the periphery of its imperial borders proved to be a harbinger of things to come. Then as now, an hegemonial drive in Europe was deterred by the guarantee pact extended by the island power to the continental states. Then, however (not, one hopes, as now), such guarantee was ignored because of its perceived frailty in the light of the discord that prevailed within the Triple Entente. But if it is easy—too easy, perhaps?—to replay the past through a redistribution of the major historical roles, it is more difficult to cast the lesser, and yet crucial, roles—to think, in short, of the Moroccos and Austria-Hungarys of the coming years.

"We imagine the past," L. B. Namier once said, "and remember the future."[7] But these memories of the future, too, are flawed. Those who have been speaking for so long of a Europe that would belong to nobody imagined too readily a Europe that had belonged to the United States in the recent past, and feared too easily a Europe that might belong to the Soviet Union in the future. But today Europe appears more determined than before to achieve more independence from the superpowers, even while it becomes more dependent on the countries of the South. The rise and self-assertiveness of the former colonies has come to haunt the former mother countries, thereby adding a new dimension to the threats and challenges raised by one superpower and then by both. Europe cannot pretend to be nationalist in the 1980s any more than the United States can pretend to be isolationist again.

Europe's Choices: Alliance's Future

Europe's Choice	Alliance's Future
L. P. Bloomfield, 1965	
1. Status quo model	Essentially as is
2. Third Force Europe	NATO dismantled; United States disengaged; USSR satisfied; a European Defense Community in the making
3. Grand Design Europe	More a Gaullist than a Kennedy Grand Design: United Europe of the Six; with nuclear forces; 3-power directorate for NATO
4. Atlantic World Model	Status quo plus, with a NATO military confederation
5. Nationalist Europe	NATO dismantled; United States isolationist, USSR "détentist"; no Europe
David P. Calleo, 1965	
1. Federalist Europe	"A very great power" as an equal partner to the United States
2. Nationalist Europe	A confederated Europe of the Six against U.S. hegemony
3. Atlantic Europe	The unification of Europe proceeds under U.S. dominance
4. Nobody's Europe	Not united, no longer dominated
Alastair Buchan, 1969	
1. Evolutionary Europe	Europe continues to evolve at the expense of NATO
2. Atlanticized Europe	U.S. dominance in all aspects of policy
3. Europe des Etats	NATO erodes but continues
4. Fragmented Europe	Every nation for itself: some states leave NATO, some stay in a modified NATO
5. Partnership Europe	NATO replaced by an alliance of two equal partners
6. Independent Federal Europe	As a balance between the United States and the USSR
Pierre Hassner, 1973	
1. A Bargained Europe	A U.S.-Soviet condominium defines the terms of the status quo in Europe
2. An Atlantic Europe	U.S. dominance in all aspects of policy
3. A Finlandized Europe	A U.S. disengagement creates the conditions for growing Soviet influence in all aspects of policy
4. A European Europe	As a balance to the United States and the USSR
W. R. Schilling et al., 1973	
1. Two-spheres Europe	Status quo
2. Sheltered Western Europe	Declining U.S. influence, but continued NATO umbrella
3. Buffered Europe	The United States and the USSR accept but supervise the normalization of the relations between East and West
4. Liberated Europe	Not only does the United States maintain its influence in western Europe, it also expands its influence in eastern Europe
5. Big Sweden Western Europe	Autonomous, strong, and nonaligned
6. Big Finland Western Europe	U.S. influence is replaced by Soviet influence
7. WEU Western Europe	Autonomous, strong, and a partner with the United States
8. Reconstituted Europe	Progressive disengagement of both the United States and the USSR, permitting a progressive reconciliation of eastern and western Europe

Note: A similar table can be found in Horst Mendershausen, *Outlook on Western Solidarity: Political Relations in the Atlantic Alliance System*, Rand Report, R–1512–PR, June 1976, pp. 10–11.

The submission of Europe to the United States has often been, to say the least, exaggerated. Early, pre-Gaullist examples of Europe's resistance to U.S. preferences abound, whether successful (as some of them were) or not. To be sure, Suez is an especially glaring expression of European impotence in the face of U.S. opposition. Yet France fought a war in Indochina against U.S. desires, and ended the conflict at the very time that the United States would have liked to see Paris continue to wage it. The Pleven Plan was proposed to defeat a U.S. proposal for the rearmament of Germany; it was rejected four years later in spite of strong U.S. pressures on its behalf. Bizerte was not shelled to satisfy U.S. imperial interests, and independence was not given by de Gaulle to Algeria to please President Kennedy. Already illusory in the 1950s, the vision of an Atlantic Europe for the future overstated U.S. capabilities and misunderstood Europe's interests as both came to be perceived in latter years. Economically, the U.S. lead has not proven to be so irrepressible as to invite further penetration, as it was expected to in earlier years. Instead, the various side effects of U.S. economic leadership have tended to encourage Europe's opposition to such penetration. Strategically, the U.S. dominance has ceased to be so overpowering as to maintain past subjugation. Instead, it has encouraged either complacency—a possible source of self-denying security—or paranoia—itself a possible source of self-induced insecurity. But both complacency and paranoia deny the United States the benefits previously accumulated through the strategic subjugation of Europe, the former because it takes U.S. protection for granted, the latter because it stresses the irrelevance and ineffectiveness of such protection. Politically, the strength of U.S. institutions has remained the envy of Europe, without, however, motivating the imitation that Washington had initially hoped for. Instead, an under-Americanization of Europe's institutions and societies has bred a sense of postindustrial malaise among leftist and rightist groups alike. In short, if there ever was a time for an Atlantic grand design—which is itself quite doubtful—this time is now gone.

A Europe that does not follow the United States will take the risk of exploding again into the many weak national pieces that comprise it, it was feared by many. But such fragmentation, too, has not taken place. Instead, the perception of a politically integrated, federalist Europe has inched closer to reality. From the beginning, the irresistible inner logic of the EEC was to be a progressive movement from the economic union of a few to the political union of all: the need to consolidate the economic gains resulting from the initial steps of the economic union, it was reasoned, would lead to further and more ambitious initiatives. In part, at least, this logic has indeed unfolded. Political parties once fearful of the consequences of European unity now support it. States once opposed to joining Europe have now acquired full membership. Opinion, once skeptical about the very idea of Europe, now applauds it. There is everywhere a European presence that is assiduously courted from within Europe (Portugal and Spain) and from without as well (associate members).

Significantly held on schedule, the direct elections of the European Parliament
have a potential that is revolutionary even if it falls far short of giving Europe a
truly supranational dimension. At the very least, the process of coordination
(among nation states and among political parties as well) will be reinforced and
accelerated to the point of irreversibility. At most, it might ultimately lead to a
transfer of power, however limited, at the expense of the council. All in all,
over the years, sacrifices of national sovereignty have been tolerated in order
to preserve or achieve gains dictated by sheer necessity.

Needless to say, the extension of such logic ad infinitum cannot be taken
for granted, and the emergence of a federalist Europe in the decade to come is
no more serious a prospect than it was a decade ago. In fact, even the possibility
of a reversal of current trends cannot be ruled out yet: throughout history,
governments have often made vital political choices at great economic cost—and
this may happen again.[8] Nor should one discount a meaningful revival of nationalist forces on the Continent. A fierce competition for markets, not only
between Europe and the United States but among European states, makes an
increasing reliance on protectionist policies all the more tempting as fragile
political coalitions find it difficult to resist effectively the various interest groups
involved. Uneven economic performances stimulate a nationalism of bitterness
for some, a nationalism of disdain for others. All too conveniently, ancient and
distorted historical caricatures can be brought back to life to explain and dismiss
one's neighbor. Thus, West Germany watches—and, at times comments on—the
maneuvering within the political system of Italy with regal amusement, even
while it warns against its economic inefficiency with marked Teutonic con-
tempt. French politicians, in the meantime, continue to find some electoral
leverage in occasional references to the new coming of a German threat, within
or without Europe, even while the government in Paris persists in using Bonn
to endow its policies with resources it might otherwise lack.

As Europe nevertheless proceeds with its unification, it reveals an identity
distinct from that of the United States. Its policies become markedly different
from those of the United States. This is not to say that there now is, or may be
soon, "a" European foreign policy. United in some areas, Europe continues to
be hopelessly divided in others. It remains, as Roger Morgan once put it, "a
strange hybrid: . . . a chameleon capable of speaking with one voice on some
matters, but hydra-headed and incapable of any sort of internal consistency or
cohesion on others."[9] Yet, on those still-all-too-rare occasions when unanimity
is secured, it often occurs in opposition to U.S. policies: at the United Nations,
for example, where nearly half of the 16 unanimous European votes registered
on the 70 political issues voted on at the General Assembly from 1970 through
1975 went against the United States.[10] In the past, all too frequently, Europeanism and Atlanticism were presented as the same thing, since the former
was to facilitate the achievements of the latter. Accordingly, conflicts between
the two were readily dismissed as a reflection of temporary personal (de Gaulle)

and national (France) stubbornness, or vain regional assertiveness that a force-ful display of U.S. power could easily control (Dulles' threat of an "agonizing reappraisal" in 1953-55; Kennedy's successful isolation of France in 1962-63; Connally's forceful economic brinksmanship in 1971-72; Kissinger's pointed linkages in 1973-75). But, while such U.S. reactions promptly restored a mea-sure of Atlantic order, they could not adequately deal with the root causes of the conflicts. Washington has often been critical of Europe's failure to unite—the main obstacle, it has been claimed, to proper Atlantic consultation, since it denies the United States a proper interlocutor. Europe's attempts to unite, how-ever, have been met with much opposition in Washington, because the inter-locutor it was thereby about to provide was not the one that had been expected. What Stanley Hoffmann aptly wrote in the summer of 1963 has continued to apply since: "The entity to which Europe's nation states are summoned [by the United States] to transfer their heritage is being duly and pressingly warned not to act as a superpower, not to establish any wall around itself, and not to give itself any preference."[11]

The search for independent European policies is, predictably, going to remain uneven and clumsy. In part, this is due to the obvious difficulties in-herent in aligning the national policies of the three major powers on the Con-tinent. Over the past 30 years, the great disputes in Europe about Europe have resulted from an attempt by one of these states to bypass either one or both of the other two: to unite Europe around an Anglo-French alliance against Ger-many; to build a supranational federal state from the Common Market against French and British objections; to unify Europe around a Franco-German axis without Great Britain. To be sure, such confrontations are far from over. Even while powerful groups within these states (the left of the Labor Party in Great Britain, some of the Socialists and most of the Gaullists in France) continued to question the most recent European initiatives (direct elections of the European parliament, for instance), their governments bid for the leadership of Europe. Yet an ever more visible *Europe des grands états* now allows attitudes common to France and Germany—and, grudgingly, Great Britain as well—to be channeled into new or stronger institutions even while the nation-state remains the center of attention and decision.

A *Europe des grands états* cautiously avoids any challenge to Soviet power in Europe, either U.S. challenge or one of its own. It does not welcome, for example, a human rights policy that is said to focus on the Soviet Union; and it trembles over the playing of a PRC card that invites an unpredictable Soviet reaction (or condones no more predictable PRC actions). In this sense, such a Europe, highly sensitized to the presence of Soviet power, faces a limited measure of Finlandization. It does not have, therefore, nor does it want to have, an eastern European policy. To approach the countries of eastern Europe directly might alienate the Soviet Union; to approach the Soviet Union first may alienate the very countries in eastern Europe (such as Rumania) likely to be most immediately responsive to western European overtures; to bypass the governments of these states altogether and give preeminence to their societies might invite a consolidation of the eastern bloc regardless of the geographic focus that such a policy of "external liberation" would adopt. In addition, an eastern European policy for western Europe would also face a problem of substance with regard to East Germany. While a united western Europe does not have to face the contradictions of a divided Germany, a uniting Europe comprising both East and West cannot ignore a Germany that would remain divided, East and West. Yet hardly any perspective would prove to be more destabilizing for Europe and for the superpowers alike than a change in the current status of the two Germanys.

Although more of a reality than ever before, Soviet power does not truly raise the fear of a direct and overt Soviet thrust through central Europe: even at a time of greater Soviet capabilities, the risk of such aggression remains as low as it probably was at a time of lesser Soviet capabilities. Whatever may be said of it, the credibility of the U.S. deterrent in Europe is not going to diminish to the point of incredibility: the Soviets are not going to overtly risk retaliation. This, however, is less true of an indirect Soviet thrust launched outside of Europe, or of a covert (political) offensive. Thus, a Soviet Union especially active at the periphery of Europe (specifically in Africa, not to mention the Middle East) can trigger a conflict that will involve and endanger Europe all the more readily as Moscow finds its own military resources more plentiful while those of its chief adversary are seen as lacking. To say that the Soviets do not take risks does not explain what constitutes a risk in the light of changing circumstances and in the eyes of a Soviet leadership that is itself about to be changed. What was rejected yesteryear as being too risky may now be said by Moscow to be safe.

The two major crises between the two superpowers have been crises born out of a Soviet misreading of U.S. intentions. In June 1950, Stalin assumed that the Truman administration, having dismissed the relevance of Korea to U.S. security, would not respond to an open and direct invasion by a regular army meant to modify a status quo supported by the United States and sponsored by the U.N. In October 1962, Khruschev assumed that the Kennedy administration, reconciled to the presence of a Communist regime 90 miles from U.S. shores, would also permit the introduction of Soviet missiles there. Actually, neither Stalin nor Khruschev truly miscalculated in either Korea or Cuba. Instead, they drew reasonable conclusions from American behavior and pronouncements prior to both crises.[12] Such behavior pointed to a similar will to compromise or even back off. At the beginning of the 1950s, this included Truman's passivity vis-à-vis contradictory strategic (the explosion of the first Soviet atomic bomb) and political (Mao's victory on the Chinese mainland) developments, as well as Truman's stated resignation to a narrow definition of U.S. security interests in the Far East (including Truman's discounting of Mao's predicted take-over in Taiwan and Acheson's famous speech at the National Press Club in January 1950). In the early 1960s, Khruschev's gamble was facilitated by the Bay of Pigs crisis, for example, when Kennedy's abstention rightly or wrongly took away any remaining possibility that the Eisenhower-sponsored effort to topple Castro might succeed after all; and by the inaction that followed the building of the Berlin wall (which required, the Kennedy administration surprisingly decided, more conciliation rather than more confrontation). In the instances of Korea and Cuba, too, Moscow expected such accommodating reaction to be facilitated by the presence of a *fait accompli*, which in effect almost came to be (the routing of the South Korean army, the near ability to make the forty-odd launching pads in Cuba operational).

At some point in the 1980s, a U.S. president will somehow need to draw the line, but such delayed reaction may dangerously be received with a measure of Soviet skepticism largely justified by the recent past. If such a confrontation takes place outside of Europe (which, save for Yugoslavia, is likely to be the case), it will meet again with bitter recrimination from a Europe that stops complaining of the United States' timidity only to complain of its recklessness. The Gaullist challenge to U.S. leadership that followed the Soviet retreat in the 1962 missile crisis aimed at separating Atlantic interests outside the Atlantic area at a moment of Soviet weakness and U.S. strength. France, it was reasoned, could develop forces that might permit the protection of such interests before Soviet capabilities were reinforced. Within a few weeks of the missile crisis, however, the Gaullist challenge was effectively controlled by the Kennedy administration because of its ability to influence Britain (at Nassau) and Germany (over the multilateral force) away from the French policies. Such influence is now questionable. Instead, a future crisis between the two superpowers (possibly at a moment of relative U.S. weakness and relative Soviet strength) might well endow the old Gaullist challenge with the very European framework it was denied previously. Faced with a similar choice between Paris and Washington, both London and, especially, Bonn may abandon the latter and follow the former. What was unthinkable in the 1960s and unlikely in the 1970s, has become quite possible for the 1980s. It is out of such a possibility that the desirability of independent European forces may regain some momentum in Europe in the years ahead. For otherwise, in the midst of the international turbulence that is accumulating for the decade to come, civilian states that have foregone military strength in favor of such civilian tools as aid and trade will find themselves progressively deprived of civilian power too.[13]

The consequences for the United States of future European initiatives in the area of independent military defense are mixed. Sharing international commitments with states that continue to hold with the United States a common vocation should be welcomed after too many years of unilateral responsibility for the preservation of world order. Yet, as has been seen, in all foreseeable circumstances, even an independently nuclear Europe will still have to be maintained within the framework of U.S. power to compensate for the relative im-

balance that can only continue to prevail within Europe between strictly continental forces. The United States may be asked, in other words, to continue to
guarantee a self-assertive competitor against a common adversary and thus vouch
for a European order, even though such an order would no longer provide the
imperial satisfactions and advantages of the past.

In any case, the Atlantic relationship has been for some time now a competitive relationship. U.S. trade negotiators must surely find it difficult to see
the evidence of a continent "astray" or "declining" in the hard and often un-
compromising bargaining of the EEC. The competition is complicated by existing and future variations in domestic situations. No longer the look-alikes of the
1950s, the European states have enlarged the boundaries of their political
spectrum to absorb parties and ideas that had been left out of the Atlantic consensual framework. For over 30 years, many in Europe thought it might be
possible to be anti-Communist without being anti-Soviet. Thus, it was not un-
common for some European governments to advocate reconciliation with Moscow while pursuing confrontation with the local Communist party. Of late,
the trend has been reversed: already, Berlinguer arouses less fear than Brezhnev,
and it is more common to display one's concern over an ascending Soviet Union—
its power if not its intentions—than it is to worry over the Communist parties
of Europe—their intentions if not their power (as most of them are declining or,
at best, stalling).

The most obvious expression of such a dislocation of the political commonalities of the Atlantic area is to be found at the level of economic policies,
in which case the future calls for more of the past tensions. As we have seen,
the competition between the United States and the countries of western Europe
for resources and markets is not new. This competition was tolerated at first by
Washington, which permitted a headstart for western Europe in capturing markets in the Communist world and in the newly independent states of Africa.
In the 1970s, the competition was fought back when Europe's denial of external markets came together with what has amounted, in fact, to a relative and
selective closing of Europe's markets to U.S. products. Although possibly the
most lucrative, arms sales is only one of several areas in which a fierce competition opposes the Europeans and the Americans, even at a time when the Europeans also compete among themselves. The Lomé Convention in the end also is
meant to gain and protect important economic advantages for Europe, possibly
at the expense of the United States. From agreement to agreement, from the
Kennedy Round to the Tokyo Round, such trade competition has escalated and
escalates more steeply as national governments become increasingly active in
trying to facilitate the opening of new markets to their own products. To add
to the trade muddle, the new competitiveness of the industrializing countries
of the Third World cuts increasingly into markets for manufactured goods in
which western European, U.S., and Japanese companies had thought they were
especially well entrenched. This new layer of international competition will

impose further strains on all sides: while formerly Europe highlighted the U.S. challenge, it is the additional challenge of the Third World that may have to be emphasized tomorrow. Meanwhile, the joint Franco-German proposal for a European Monetary System (EMS)—already significant politically since it represents an active expression of West Germany's exasperation with U.S. policies— might effectively encourage more intra-European trade at the expense of outsiders that are not "associated" with the system. In due time, this may cause the emergence of two competitive regional groupings for the West: one, centered on the EEC, would primarily want to attract through various trade preferences those East European, African, Middle Eastern, and sterling area countries whose trade relations and political orientations are primarily and traditionally European; the other, centered on the United States and Japan, might primarily embrace the Western hemisphere and the Pacific area, including the PRC.[14]

Going beyond and feeding the realities of Atlantic discord on such a multitude of issues, it is all too convenient for Europe's political leadership to charge the United States with the responsibility of an overall malaise, if not crisis, at home and throughout the world. After 25 years of steady expansion with near full employment and relatively stable prices, the slowdown of the 1970s finds a facile explanation in past and present U.S. economic policies. After nearly three decades of security achieved on the basis of U.S. military superiority, the uncertainties of the future find a ready explanation in the past misuses of U.S. power and the present deterioration of U.S. will. Undoubtedly, such charges are not, as we have seen, wholly unjustified. For the United States, therefore, the task ahead is to restore in Europe some measure of confidence in U.S. domestic and foreign policies. Already questioned in a previous era of U.S. economic and military dominance over allies and adversaries alike, U.S. credibility clearly becomes even more compromised at a time when such dominance is being overtly challenged, not only by the adversaries but by the allies as well. Thus, Europe's on-going choices—enlargement, Lomé, the European parliament, EMS—add up into a whole that reflects a growing will to go along without—if not against—the United States. Such choices, however, remain tentative. For western Europe, therefore, the task is still to agree at last on what it wants, how, and when. For too many years, the Europeans have wanted to have it both ways: rejecting the dollar while hoarding it; criticizing the nuclear umbrella while staying carefully under it; disapproving of U.S. leadership when exerted, but regretting it when withdrawn. For all, the task is to adjust to an alliance that continues to evolve into an ever more flexible coalition, whose membership fluctuates, and in the midst of which interallied diplomacy increasingly takes the form of adversary relationships calling for trade-offs over military, economic, and political issues: for the United States, the trade-off between policies that permit the necessary satisfaction of national goals on the one hand and policies that promote the long-run viability of an orderly international system on the other; for the Europeans, a trade-off between the imperatives of interdependence on the one hand and the desired regional and national autonomy on the other.

In short, the highly effective policies that were devised in 1947–49 apply to the world of the late 1970s even less than they applied to the world of the late 1960s, as neither the conceptualization of defense strategies, the coordination of economic objectives, nor the synchronization of political aspirations now appears to be feasible within the existing Atlantic structures. The challenge of the 1980s, then, will be to rebuild these structures in such a way as to avoid Atlantic anarchy, which would be detrimental to all. That these structures will have to be devised within an international system that is itself in a state of flux taxes even further the imagination and the creativity of those who will share the responsibility for containing and reversing the erosion of the alliance.

NOTES

1. George Liska, *Europe Ascendant: The International Politics of Unification* (Baltimore: Johns Hopkins Press, 1964), pp. 169–170.

2. Stanley Hoffmann, "Fragments Floating in the Here and Now," *Daedalus*, Winter 1979, p. 3. Also see Walter Laqueur's *A Continent Astray, 1970–1978* (New York: Oxford University Press, 1979) as compared with his earlier *Europe Since Hitler* (New York: Weidenfeld and Nicolson, 1970).

3. Roy Prosterman, *Surviving to 3000: An Introduction to the Study of Lethal Conflict* (Belmont, California: Duxbury Press, 1972); Robert Hunter, "Power and Peace," *Foreign Policy*, Winter 1972–73, p. 38; Edmund Stillman et al., *L'Envol de la France dans les Années 80* (Paris: Hackette, 1973); Herman Kahn, *The Emerging Japanese Superstate, Challenge and Response* (Englewood Cliffs, N.J.: Prentice Hall, 1970).

4. Louis Halle, "The Cracked Alliance," *New Republic*, February 23, 1963, pp. 17–20; Henry Kissinger, *The Troubled Partnership* (New York: McGraw Hill, 1966); David Calleo, *The Atlantic Fantasy: The U.S., NATO, and Europe* (Baltimore: Johns Hopkins Press, 1970); Irving Kristol, "NATO: The End of an Era," *The Wall Street Journal*, November 16, 1973; Robert Pfaltzgraff, *The Atlantic Community: A Complex Imbalance* (New York: Van Nostrand Reinhold, 1969); Robert Shaetzel, *The Unhinged Alliance: America and the European Community* (New York: Harper & Row, 1975).

5. Warner R. Schilling, et al., *American Arms and a Changing Europe: Dilemmas of Deterrence and Disarmament* (New York: Columbia University Press, 1973), pp. 120–21.

6. Lincoln P. Bloomfield, *Western Europe 1965–1975: Five Scenarios* (Bendix Corporation, April 1, 1965); David P. Calleo, *Europe's Future: The Grand Alternatives* (New York: Norton, 1965); Alastair Buchan, *Europe's Futures, Europe's Choices: Models of Western Europe in the 1970s* (New York: Columbia University Press, 1969); Pierre Hassner, *Europe in the Age of Negotiations*, The Washington Papers, vol. 1, no. 8 (Beverly Hills and London: Sage Publications, 1973); Schilling et al., op. cit.

7. Quoted in Roger Hillsman, *The Crouching Future: International Politics and U.S. Foreign Policy: A Forecast* (New York: Doubleday, 1975), p. 233.

8. Calleo, *Europe's Future*, op. cit., pp. 64–65.

9. Roger P. Morgan, *High Politics, Low Politics: Toward a Foreign Policy for Western Europe*, The Washington Papers, vol. 1, No. 11 (Beverly Hills and London: Sage Publications, 1973), p. 6.

10. Mendershausen, op. cit., p. 91.

11. Stanley Hoffmann, "Discord in Community," in *The Atlantic Community*, ed. Francis O. Wilcox and H. Field Haviland (New York: Frederick A. Praeger, 1964), pp. 3–31.

12. James L. Payne, *The American Threat: The Fear of War as an Instrument of Foreign Policy* (Chicago: Markham, 1970), p. 47.

13. Harold van Buren Cleveland, "How the Dollar Standard Died," *Foreign Policy*, Winter 1971–72, p. 51.

14. Francois Duchene, "A New European Defense Community," *Foreign Affairs*, October 1971, pp. 69–82. See also Hassner, op. cit., p. 26.

ABOUT THE AUTHOR

SIMON SERFATY is the Director of the Washington Center of Foreign Policy Research, The Johns Hopkins University School of Advanced International Studies. His other books include *The Elusive Enemy* and *France, de Gaulle, and Europe.*